T0328676

Cambridge Elements

Elements in Religion and Monotheism
edited by
Paul K. Moser
Loyola University Chicago
Chad Meister
*Affiliate Scholar, Ansari Institute for Global Engagement with Religion,
University of Notre Dame*

MONOTHEISM AND DIVINE AGGRESSION

Collin Cornell
Fuller Theological Seminary

CAMBRIDGE
UNIVERSITY PRESS

Shaftesbury Road, Cambridge CB2 8EA, United Kingdom

One Liberty Plaza, 20th Floor, New York, NY 10006, USA

477 Williamstown Road, Port Melbourne, VIC 3207, Australia

314–321, 3rd Floor, Plot 3, Splendor Forum, Jasola District Centre, New Delhi – 110025, India

103 Penang Road, #05–06/07, Visioncrest Commercial, Singapore 238467

Cambridge University Press is part of Cambridge University Press & Assessment, a department of the University of Cambridge.

We share the University's mission to contribute to society through the pursuit of education, learning and research at the highest international levels of excellence.

www.cambridge.org
Information on this title: www.cambridge.org/9781009454421

DOI: 10.1017/9781009067171

© Collin Cornell 2023

This publication is in copyright. Subject to statutory exception and to the provisions of relevant collective licensing agreements, no reproduction of any part may take place without the written permission of Cambridge University Press & Assessment.

When citing this work, please include a reference to the DOI 10.1017/9781009067171

First published 2023

A catalogue record for this publication is available from the British Library.

ISBN 978-1-009-45442-1 Hardback
ISBN 978-1-009-06589-4 Paperback
ISSN 2631-3014 (online)
ISSN 2631-3006 (print)

Cambridge University Press & Assessment has no responsibility for the persistence or accuracy of URLs for external or third-party internet websites referred to in this publication and does not guarantee that any content on such websites is, or will remain, accurate or appropriate.

Monotheism and Divine Aggression

Elements in Religion and Monotheism

DOI: 10.1017/9781009067171
First published online: December 2023

Collin Cornell
Fuller Theological Seminary
Author for correspondence: Collin Cornell, collincornell@fuller.edu

Abstract: The aggression of the biblical God is notorious. The phrase "Old Testament God" conjures up images of jealousy and wrath, smiting and judging. But is it only an accident that this god became capital-G God, the unique creator and sustainer of three world religions? Or is there a more substantive connection between monotheism and divine aggression? This Element proposes exactly this causal connection. In three case studies, it showcases ways that literarily treating one god alone as god amplifies divine destructiveness. This happens according to two dynamics: God absorbs the destructive power of other divine beings – and God monopolizes divinity such that other beings, even special ones like God's beloved king or the people of God, are rendered vulnerable to divine aggression. The Element also attends to the literary contexts and counterbalances within which the Hebrew Bible imagines divine aggression.

Keywords: monotheism, biblical theology, Hebrew Bible, ancient Near East, divine wrath

© Collin Cornell 2023

ISBNs: 9781009454421 (HB), 9781009065894 (PB), 9781009067171 (OC)
ISSNs: 2631-3014 (online), 2631-3006 (print)

Contents

1 Introduction

This is an Element about monotheism and divine aggression. More specifically, it makes an argument about the relation of the one, monotheism, to the other, aggression. The relation this Element proposes is that of cause and effect. Simply put, the Element claims that monotheism, or, as the case may be, *monotheizing*, makes the profile of the singular, mono-god *more aggressive*. The aggression of the god in question (the biblical god) is notorious: the phrase "Old Testament God" conjures up images of jealousy and wrath, smiting and judging. The present work doesn't so much deny this impression as reframe it. By drawing texts about the biblical god alongside depictions of other gods, the Element aims to show that the biblical god is more aggressive than they are. His intensified destructiveness results from the Bible's elevation of one god to supremacy.

This is, it should be clear, a theological argument, but only in the nontechnical sense that it concerns God, gods, and their descriptions. According to a more restrictive or technical definition, the Element is not theological, since it does not make an overt or sustained proposal about who God – the real, extratextual, living God – is, or about how current-day religious communities should comport themselves in relation to him. The Element's ambit is, instead, historical and comparative: it considers the Bible as an ancient document alongside other writings from antiquity, and it ranges the biblical god alongside his divine neighbors. It is in recognition of the Bible as an artifact, and hence, too, of the god the Bible narrates, praises, and pleads to, that the present work lowercases "god" throughout. Whatever else the biblical god is, he is a character within the texts of Hebrew Scripture, and so comparable to gods preserved in other texts from the ancient world.

As is always the case, though, when writing about the biblical god, theological currents and convictions flow beneath the surface. Inherited words, expectations, and affects circulate in the chthonic realm of the author's psyche, in disciplinary conventions, and in the cultural ether. Even while observing a historical stricture – striving neutrally to notice what data emerge through the exercise of juxtaposing the Bible with other historical realia – scholars often lapse into a theologically defensive or a theologically critical posture. They subtly promote the biblical god out of crypto-devotion, or they subtly war against him out of crypto-indignation at his long legacy, which has proven harmful for so many human lives. The present Element cannot transcend such slipstreams and undertows. But as a preliminary step toward the postbiblical career of the biblical god's aggression, each of its sections takes care to include literary contexts and counterbalances. That is, even as the Element demonstrates the amplified aggressiveness of the biblical god relative to other, textualized gods, it presents moments from the reception of the biblical texts in question. These interpretations of Yhwh's aggression could fall under either of the above headings: whether out of religious loyalty or out of religious critique, they recontextualize and reconfigure the god's destructive power.[1]

To put a finer point on it: at specific times and under specific intellectual pressures, not all of which are recoverable, biblical writers concentrated divine powers into one god. This god, the god named Yhwh, therefore speaks and acts destructively, and in fact *very* destructively, given that divine destructiveness is not, for the most part, deputized in the Bible to some other under-god. Nothing and no one is safe from Yhwh's destructiveness, because Yhwh alone enjoys the unshakable favor and safety inhering to divinity. But – and here is the finer point – this particular way of distributing divine aggression (or divine privilege) did not persuade all the inheritors of the biblical god. Whether devotion to Yhwh motivated them, or repugnance at some of Yhwh's biblical conduct, or both – or neither, and it was simply a change of overall intellectual regime – subsequent "Yahwists," both Jews and Christians, relaxed the biblical concentration of all divine powers into one god. The sections that follow track this interpretive development, and in this fashion they yield up fodder for sympathetic and indignant current-day readers alike.

In addition to being theological, historical, and comparative, the argument of the present Element mobilizes two further looming and troublesome concepts: monotheism and divine aggression. The first is troublesome because it is supersaturated. An immense literature addresses the rise of monotheism (or initial lack thereof) in ancient Israel, not to mention other enormous literatures that treat the viability of the concept for ongoing and constructive use. To gain any purchase, the present Element must winnow and clarify what it means by this fraught term. The second concept, divine aggression, suffers from an equal and opposite problem: it is unknown, even idiosyncratic. The angriness of the biblical god is nearly a cliché, a generic half-truth scattered culturally far and wide (think again of the biblical god's popular reputation for smiting and judging). But "divine aggression" is not, at present, a phrase with any specific, programmatic value in academic discourse, whether of biblical studies, ancient Near Eastern studies, or theology more broadly. It, too, must receive a working definition, to save it from obscurity. Parts of the present section attempt just that, a twofold definition of terms. In closing, the present section provides a thumbnail sketch of the arguments that following Element sections build out.

---

[1] For the same reason as with the book's capitalization of "god," namely, to despecialize and thereby to make it more accessible for comparison with other gods, the book also lowercases the four-lettered divine name Yhwh.

Monotheism

"Monotheism" is, by common definition, the belief that there is only one god. Such belief subsists in the mind, or perhaps somewhere else in the human interior, but, at any rate, it identifies assent rather than, say, observable practice or performance. The content of that belief may also be rounded out. Affirming that there is only one god entails that other gods are not just off limits, neither are they merely subordinate, but that they do not exist at all. God alone is God.

This much seems almost commonsensical: monotheism = one + god + ism. And yet in spite of its wide reception, several problems accrue to this concept in its application to the Bible. First, there is the issue of anachronism. Monotheism is not a concept indigenous to the Bible's own self-presentation. Rather, the term appears in English only from the seventeenth century onward. This means that wielding monotheism to gauge biblical texts risks shoehorning and even distorting the data. In a sense, though, this is a trivial concern, or at least a generic one. Many or most of the concepts that biblical scholars ply are postbiblical, anachronistic, and hence potentially distortive.

The more serious mismatch that "monotheism" poses is this: it is *intellectualizing*. To put it crudely, monotheism happens in the head; it is a philosophical proposition about the absolute number of gods. The term debuted as a tool to categorize religions: quite apart from their own self-conceptions, or the messy worlds of ethnicity, scripture, and ritual, the seventeenth-century English Platonists who invented "monotheism" used it to isolate one decisive and discriminating factor, an intellectual one: the asserted population of god(s). If, according to such-and-such religions, there was only ultimately one god, those religions are monotheistic; if more than one, then polytheistic.

The concept of monotheism thus sieves out an intellectual credendum from the religious river sludge (so to speak) that actually contains it. Note that this operation of separating out an intellectual proposition works regardless of the significance given by a religious tradition itself to such subscription, whether or not one-god-belief is a major focus of liturgy, prayer, or self-identity on the part of real religionists, or the particular rhetorical ends to which their confession of one god alone contributes. R. W. L. Moberly summarily articulates the problem:

> "Monotheism" in the 17th century entailed a certain intellectualizing whereby believing in one god becomes assent to the proposition that the class of deity has only one member ... rather than a kind of transformative and demanding awareness of reality that is rooted in, and inseparable from, a range of moral disciplines and symbolic practices [the religious river sludge!].[2]

---

[2] Moberly, "How Appropriate Is Monotheism?" 221–222.

When it comes to biblical texts that appear to profess the sole deity of Yhwh, the mismatch is acute. Whatever else the latter chapters of Isaiah are doing, for example, they are not primarily launching a philosophical point. When the Book of Isaiah declares on behalf of Yhwh, "I am Yhwh, and there is no other; besides me there is no god" (45:5a), its rhetorical purpose is not to retally the number of gods. Rather, this text and others like it seek to induce the sort of transformation and demand that Moberly mentions. They reassure and challenge the people of Israel. Interpreting a passage like this one as "monotheistic" – believing in but one god – can misdirect attention from what the prophet's claim more holistically attempts.

The intellectualizing of "monotheism" abstracts from the existential and moral concerns within which any textual case of one-god-ism is embedded. It *also* loses traction on the particular recipients and transmitters of professions about one god. To return to the example of Isaiah: not only does this prophetic book aim at something other than intellectual subscription, it also aims specifically and programmatically *at Israel*. By design, however, "monotheism" is a category that transcends individual religious traditions; it stands outside of them and organizes them in a taxonomy. But this trans-religious intent differs radically from the communicative goal of the biblical texts that are oftentimes labeled monotheistic. The latter belong integrally to the relationship between Yhwh and Israel. To quote Robert Goldenberg:

> Even when uttering apparently global claims on Yhwh's behalf, the biblical writers may not have intended that those claims be understood globally. The world in Isaiah's time was not yet familiar with the notion of universal religion, the notion that a religious truth ought to be true everywhere and at all times.[3]

In these ways, the problem of anachronism acquires more particularity and bite. The intellectualizing and universalizing features of "monotheism" misalign with the existential holism and national specificity of biblical texts. Sifting texts of Hebrew Scripture with this criterion could thereby mislead. Monotheism may then be, as some scholars have argued, a device unfit to plumb biblical literature.[4] But anachronism is not the only or even the most pressing drawback. There is also a more practical limitation: most of what modern researchers have to work with is ancient *texts*; and such texts relate obliquely at best to what ancient persons thought, believed, and felt, let alone the larger communities of which ancient scribes were members. In other words, even if it could be proven that Isaiah 45 asserts a would-be universal truth (that there is only one god), this would not guarantee that the prophet or scribe who

---

[3] Goldenberg, "Why Should the Look-Alikes Be a Problem?" 90.
[4] Fredriksen, "Mandatory Retirement," 241–243.

first wrote the chapter's words held exactly to such a belief, nor that they held to it as an ongoing, inward conviction. Even less so would it automatically entail that the chapter's addressees accepted its monotheistic claim. Rather, *textual evidence* simply and solely authorizes arguments about *textual rhetoric*.[5]

To some readers of the present Element, this practical limitation might appear too cautious, even impractically so. If a prophetic persona in the Bible says that there is only one god, someone aback of the text must have really believed that! This makes sense as an inference. But with regard to the Bible, it is often, even usually, difficult to locate the ancient persons responsible for composing the text. Biblical passages lack a caption; there is not for them a colophon as in some texts from the ancient city of Ugarit, when the scribe named Ilimilku declares, "I wrote this!" Even in biblical writings associated with an individual prophet such as Isaiah, much of the material under his name does not trace back to the historical personality. It requires some speculation to identify what person or persons behind the Bible could have espoused its occasional expressions of one-god-belief, if that is what they are.[6]

Without secure access to an individual *behind* the text, it still seems like a sound extrapolation that a community *in front of* the text must have supported its theology sufficiently to preserve and pass it along. Even if we must remain tentative about pinpointing monotheism to the psyche of one or another exilic (or postexilic) prophets who took up the name and mantle of Isaiah of Jerusalem, surely scholars are justified to think that some among the book's recipients affirmed its high declarations that Yhwh alone is god and there is none besides him; otherwise they would not have taken pains to transmit these prolix oracles! This much is academically prudent. *Someone* agreed with Isaiah's theology, or respected his authority. But who or how many or in what ways? Any but the vaguest further claim quickly runs up against the limits imposed by relevant data.

The previous part of the section already mentioned the fact that postbiblical Jewish and Christian traditions relaxed the biblical concentration of divine powers into one god, Yhwh. But this same history of reception adds a further caution to the attempt at leveraging biblical texts for insight into the beliefs of persons and communities that produced and circulated them. Isaiah and its bold Yhwh-alone declarations were copied and quoted numerously by ancient Jewish writers: the Dead Sea Scrolls, the apostle Paul, the New Testament evangelists. Yet all these writers also rather unselfconsciously treat other gods as real. Powers,

---

[5] The present study has learned from Mark Smith's emphasis on monotheistic *discourse* (*Origins of Biblical Monotheism*, 151–166).

[6] On Ilimilku, see, inter alia, Wyatt, "The Evidence of the Colophons"; on the contrasting anonymity, even "self-subsumption," of the Bible's authors and editors, Chapman, *Law and the Prophets*, 99–104.

principalities, angels, archangels, and the heavenly temple itself – even "gods," directly and as such – populate these writings. For them the monotheizing literary template of Hebrew Scripture did not preclude active belief, practice, and literary production assuming a multiplicity of divine beings.[7]

Other texts *within Isaiah itself* depict the reality and reach of divine beings besides Yhwh: the mythic sea dragon over whom Yhwh triumphs (Isa 51:9), the heavenly host at his service (Isa 40:1–8, 25–26; 45:12).[8] These examples suggest that texts we might otherwise identify as monotheistic can accomplish something *rhetorically* that does not necessarily coincide with a behind-the-text belief that Yhwh is the only god who exists. Once more, for purpose of the present Element, the most trustworthy arguments are calibrated to the nature of the evidence: observations about the *rhetoric* of texts fit their profile *as texts* and do not seek to reach through them and beyond them into the world of belief, of the texts' authors or their first readers.

As such, the procedure of the present Element is primarily textual. It reads biblical texts and compares them with other, ancient texts, and it pays attention to the rhetorical workings of these texts. Insofar as monotheism remains a useful conceptual tool for such a historical and comparative project, it must fit within these coordinates. And so the present Element defines monotheism *away from belief*. Instead of an intellectualizing or "heady" assent to a universal, trans-religious proposition about the numeration of gods, it takes monotheism as a textual phenomenon: a specific way of depicting gods "on the page." Perhaps counterintuitively, the definition of monotheism this Element uses does not center on their absolute number. Narrating or discoursing about only one god is *not* what makes a text monotheistic; neither does narrating or discoursing about multiple gods necessarily render a text polytheistic. This Element's definition of monotheism instead hinges on *the (textual) distribution of divine powers*.

For texts that are monotheistic, or better, texts that monotheize, other forces, fates, and powers in the universe ultimately answer to one god. The one god is not shown negotiating with them, praying to an older god, pursuing magical rituals, seeking to discover an already-established divine destiny. Odd as it may sound to readers familiar with a monotheistic frame of reference, all of these were live possibilities in ancient writings. Texts about Greek and Mesopotamian gods portray them as praying and working magic. They are also beholden to fate, a prior, "primal, meta-divine realm."[9] Even if the power of such praying and fate-bound gods vastly exceeds human power, there are yet deeper divine

---

[7] See Smith: "biblical claims of monotheism are generally rhetorical" (*Origins of Biblical Monotheism*, 154).

[8] See Olyan, "Is Isaiah 40–55 Really Monotheistic?"

[9] Lawson, *Concept of Fate in Ancient Mesopotamia*, 39, quoted in Chapman, "*Miqreh* and Yhwh," 188.

powers to which they, too, report. Such texts are polytheistic in the sense that sovereignty is, at bottom, pluriform.

By contrast, monotheizing texts aggregate divine powers into one god.[10] These texts may tell about many divine beings and their goings-on, but the sub-gods do not truly stand over against the one god. That god, the supreme god, may conscript them at his discretion, or destroy them at will. The one god holds the others in existence or wills them into nonexistence. Or, even more radically than creating or decreating, commanding or extinguishing, some ancient texts consider lesser gods as extensions or manifestations of the one god. Their agency and over-againstness is yet more reduced. Thus, for example, at least one Late Babylonian text claims about several major traditional gods that they are but names for the high god, Marduk.[11] Even if it refers to multiple gods, a text like that one *monotheizes* in that it concentrates divine powers into one god.

As Benjamin Sommer has written, "distinguishing between monotheism and polytheism involves not counting divine beings but studying the relations among them."[12] For the present Element, these relations are not behind the text in the minds of antique writers, but available from their written word; and, to note, the exercise of distinguishing monotheism and polytheism is internal to the Jewish and Christian traditions. Biblical texts monotheize – but not all of them, and not in the same way – and postbiblical Jewish or Christian texts de-monotheize, redistributing divine powers away from a sole, central sovereign; and all this must be discerned through close scrutiny of just how these texts present god(s).

Divine Aggression

The second titular term the present section must define is "divine aggression." Whereas monotheism is much discussed, divine aggression has no particular standing in scholarship on the Bible or the ancient Near East. If there is any keyword to which specialized studies *have* dedicated attention, it is to "divine wrath" or "divine anger." Both of these terms have received a number of book-length investigations in recent decades, and these have advanced the discussion.[13]

The advantage of these works is their lexical discipline. They focus on vocabulary for "anger" in biblical and other literature, and this lends

---

[10] This definition of monotheizing differs from another prominent exemplar, namely, James Sanders's (*Monotheizing Process*), which posits not an innertextual phenomenon but rather a process that lies behind the production of texts – and which modern-day religious communities might reprise.

[11] Lambert, *Babylonian Creation Myths*, 265.

[12] Sommer, "Yehezkel Kaufmann and Recent Scholarship," 205.

[13] Grant, *Divine Anger in the Hebrew Bible*; Wälchli, *Gottes Zorn in den Psalmen*; Baloian, *Anger in the Old Testament*; also Kratz and Spieckermann, eds., *Divine Wrath and Divine Mercy*. See also Berges, "Zorn Gottes" and Considine, "Theme of Divine Wrath."

their treatments a certain helpful selectivity. Because words for "anger" in Hebrew and other languages describe an affective state, it means the theology of these studies – in the general and nontechnical sense of theology outlined earlier – also remains at the level of affect.

Anger or wrath is a divine *emotion*. To be sure, the commonest Hebrew word for anger refers to *the nose*, which is an observable, outward, physiological referent rather than a feeling on the interior of a person. Several other relevant Hebrew lexemes for anger denote *burning*, sometimes with regard to the heat of an angry face and other times to the heat of tumultuous emotion. As Matthew Schlimm notes, however, the dominant metaphors for anger in the Hebrew Bible (ANGER IS A NOSE; ANGER IS HEAT) are *dead* metaphors.[14] They do not summon images of the face or of fire but designate the affect of anger in a more commonplace, shopworn way. Other studies, especially Deena Grant's, show that the divine emotion of anger comes to textual expression in response to stimuli that can be enumerated, and that the affect has a social dimension. Nonetheless, inasmuch as these books stay anchored in Hebrew words for "anger," they orbit the affective.

This lexical discipline presents a disadvantage. As Schlimm says in his review of Deena Grant's book, "many biblical texts appear to have anger implicitly present, even though a lexical term for anger is missing."[15] Selectivity provides control, but it means many relevant data are left out, and the total analysis of the biblical god is less fulsome. Furthermore, even expanding one's investigation to include implicit anger still keeps affect as the defining parameter. And, for as well represented as divine anger is in texts across the Bible, it may be that texts *showing* the deity's destructive activities are more widespread than texts *telling* of the deity's affect. To state it differently, the harms caused by Yhwh offer a far larger category in Hebrew Scripture than do texts about his emotion of anger (whether explicit or implicit). For example, the downfall of the two kingdoms, Israel and Judah, and their expulsion from the Land is a basic horizon for much of the Primary History, also much of the Prophets – even apart from occurrences of words specifically communicating divine anger.

This is, so far, simply a quantitative argument: that divine destructiveness engages a lot more passages than does divine anger considered as an affect. But the direction of argument reflects a deeper theological possibility: that ancient texts, the Bible included, reflect interest primarily in the divine *impact* on human lives rather than inward divine affect or intention – the *behavior* of gods rather than their *motivation*. The former (impact) was far more observable

---

[14] Schlimm, *From Fratricide to Forgiveness*, 82.
[15] Schlimm, Review of Deena Grant, *Divine Anger in the Hebrew Bible*.

than the latter (motivation). Any number of biblical texts could be called to witness to this phenomenological priority. All the psalms that ask God "why?" or "how long?" are convinced that God is doing something, or willfully not doing something; divine *action* is a real, lived experience. It is the divine *motive* that is (painfully) inscrutable.

Or again, a few biblical texts present a control case, instances where the same event is attributed to divine anger in one place but to some other divine happenstance in another. In 2 Sam 24:1, "the anger of Yhwh was kindled against Israel [literally: the nose of Yhwh burned] and he incited David against them, saying, 'Go, count the people of Israel and Judah.'" Yet in 1 Chr 21:1, a literary redux of the same story, the inspiration to number the people arises from a different source. The verse reads: "Satan stood up against Israel, and incited David to count the people of Israel." The fixed point in the narrative is the outward event of the census. The destructive divine effect is nonnegotiable. What is revisable, which is to say less fixed, is the divine psyche aback of the census, or, in this example, *whose* divine psyche. (This verse also gives an early, innerbiblical example of relaxing the concentration of all divine powers into Yhwh.)

If this priority of the outward holds true across various genres within biblical and related literatures, it entails that the scholarly project of rendering a profile of divine *anger* selects for something that may not be the foremost concern of the texts in question. Biblical writings that describe Yhwh's wrath likely do not do so out of an intellectual or spiritual interest. Rather, they believe that Yhwh's wrath *lands* in some form or fashion that is only too detectable in human lives. The writers yield up words about divine affect because that affect threatens to spill over into destructive effect, or it has already done so. It is in a way the theological inverse of Melanchthon's saying: "to know Christ is to know his benefits." To know Yhwh is to know his destructions – the concrete, observable manifestations of the divine will rather than a scholastic account of that will in its hidden movements and motives.[16]

For understanding biblical and other antique writings, divine destructiveness is a much more populous category than divine anger; it may also have some conceptual and existential priority, in that even texts about anger have actual or potential destructiveness in view. These two arguments recommend destructiveness as a heurism, especially for a comparison of gods-in-texts such as the present Element pursues. Taking destructive impacts rather than destructive passions in hand enables us to consider a fuller repertoire of texts, and perhaps it

---

[16] On the relative proportion of destructiveness to benefits, at least in one biblical poem, see Strawn, "Yhwh's Poesie." On challenges of defining aggression, destructiveness, and violence, see Tolan, "Understanding Violence" and Walker, *Power of Images*, 27–29.

lends more purchase on the rhetoric of these texts, since in their cajoling, threatening, inviting, and praising, divinely wrought *harm* looms large. It is a pervasive anxiety, which some texts strategically pique and others pacify.

Divine destructiveness – or to use another word, aggression – is hence a wider and a deeper classification than divine anger or wrath. Texts that show gods enacting harm upon humans (or nonhumans) are numerous and variegated, and may tap into a primordial human worry vis-à-vis gods. As such, the present work cannot rely on a lexical discipline; no particular suite of words identifies *aggression*. Prayers and rituals and stories that invoke it draw on many terms for killing, fighting, and afflicting. And indeed, if such texts provide any insight into the *motives* for harmful divine behavior, they may refer to other emotions besides anger. The next section discusses the biblical Flood Story, which is a premier example of divine destructiveness: God blots out all life, releasing the creation back into its primeval, watery chaos. But in terms of affect, *anger is absent*. Yhwh is not enraged. He is *grieved*: "Yhwh was sorry that he had made humankind on the earth, and it grieved him to his heart" (Gen 6:6). An analysis of divine anger would pass over this narrative; an analysis of divine aggression must take it into account.

In addition to these two strengths of focusing on divine destructiveness – it opens more materials for comparison, and it more directly engages the anxieties that textual rhetorics activate – there is one further consideration that reinforces the present Element's approach. As seen earlier, the Element's working definition of monotheism pertains to the textual distribution of divine powers, and its main proposal is that divine aggression amounts to one such power, which monotheizing texts build into the one divine self rather than leaving in a truly multipolar shape. Questions may remain about what precisely constitutes a "divine power" and what qualifies aggression for membership in that category. But if these terms are fuzzy, they at least enable the possibility of tracking reconfigurations of the divine across various ancient texts. To return in advance to the Flood Story: in its Mesopotamian versions, one god initiates destruction of the world by water, and another god works to save the flood hero and conserve life. By contrast, in the biblical version, one god plays both the destructive *and* the recreative roles. However we label it, the aggressive "part" in the story – the capacity to destroy – *is* transferable, because it was transferred. A discernible characterological contribution, a complement of specific (diluvian) activities, is allocated here to one agent and there to another.

The same cannot be said of divine *anger*. Its profile, especially under a lexical or terminological discipline, is far slimmer: it designates an affect, and does not necessarily bundle it together with character, incident, and all the rest that goes into a part or power. As such, anger or wrath makes for too punctiliar an instrument to track with across literatures. Anger is nontransferable; different characters experience anger episodically, but because of that punctiliar quality, anger cannot aggregate into one divine persona. No character can "hog" anger: both Yhwh and Moses become enraged at Israel, for example – but noncompetitively, at different narrative moments. A role or capacity, however, because it integrates a constellation of features in an ongoing or unrepeatable way, may admit of only one agent in a given text. For comparing the impacts of monotheism on literary presentations of deity, the latter, larger, looser category is therefore preferable.

Therapeutic Aggression?

The present work selects for divine aggression that results in harm to humans and human communities. It defines aggression as more or less identical to divine destructiveness, and it attends to the anxieties about divine potential to harm that various ancient texts deliberately provoke. It deserves notice, however, that a few biblical texts – a minority report, perhaps – narrate events of divine damage whose purpose is *therapeutic*. That is to say: although the divine actions they narrate eventuate in *injury*, the biblical text frames them positively or purgatively.

One example of this might be the mysterious text of Genesis 32, Jacob wrestling at Peniel. The "man" in the story strove with Jacob all night but did not prevail over him, and so "struck him on the hip socket," putting it out of joint (v. 25). Jacob limps away from the encounter (v. 31b). And yet it was a place of seeing God's face, hence the name *Peniel* (Hebrew for *face of God*, v. 30), and it was a moment of blessing. The damage and the blessing are bound up in the same narrated event. The Israelites honor the holiness of this damaging blessing and blessed damage by refraining from eating the thigh muscle. An approach oriented to divine anger would rightfully pass over this story. No character, neither the man nor Jacob, is *angry*. But it does belong to a discussion of divine *aggression*, since the "man" shows divine powers and prerogatives – he says Jacob has "struggled with God" (v. 28b New King James Version (NKJV)), and Jacob says he has seen God face to face (v. 30b) – and the man effects permanent harm to Jacob's body.

Or again, the example of Isaiah's "call" story: in chapter 6, he sees Yhwh within the temple, surrounded by angelic attendants who call "holy, holy, holy" (v. 3). In response to this sight, Isaiah cries out: "Woe is me! I am lost, for I am a man of unclean lips, and I live among a people of unclean lips, yet my eyes have seen the King, Yhwh of Hosts!" (v. 5). One of the seraphs (in Hebrew, *burning ones*) flew down to him; having taken a live coal from the altar, it touches Isaiah's mouth with it. The narrative gives no indication of Isaiah's pain. But we might well infer it from the seraph's interpretation that immediately follows: "Now that this has touched your lips, your guilt has departed and your sin is blotted out" (v. 7b). This is no painless process, but rather a purgation in preparation for Isaiah's ministry. It is a story of divine harm – but to salutary effect.

The present work must acknowledge the presence of such episodes in Hebrew Scripture: texts that tell of divine aggression, even violence, but that do not simply or solely kick up fear. Rather, they situate divinely caused harms within a larger divine intention of blessing, preparation, and purgation. But these texts will not directly intersect its main argument about the relationship of monotheizing to divine aggression. Only the concluding section revisits the question of therapeutic aggression, set against a larger constructive frame. In the meanwhile, solely reading and exegesis of individual passages can determine the rhetorical uses to which divine aggression is put.

Argument of the Work

Monotheism and Divine Aggression traces the effects of the one phenomenon, monotheism, on the second, divine aggression. Its basic argument is that by monopolizing aggression, the biblical god becomes *more* aggressive relative to his ancient, textual congeners. But this monopoly has another and symmetrical effect. Characters (or "parts") who in other literary contexts possess their own autonomy and agency, their own self-determination, are reduced and placed at the discretion of the one god.

The argument of the present work thus unfolds in two directions. First, it exposits monotheizing in its *aggregative* or combinatory appearance. Section 2 examines the Genesis Flood Story to show how the biblical god has absorbed the divine roles of several Mesopotamian gods, including all their acts of unmaking and destruction, but also, and especially with a view to the mother goddess Nintu, their grief and regret. Her "part" in the drama is transferred into him. He is left as the sole divine actor, and a more complex and aggressive one at that.

Second, the book inspects monotheizing in its *evacuative* form: Section 3 looks at Yhwh's presentation in Psalm 89. There he assaults and aggresses another character who is, in other, similar royal texts, absolutely safe from the god's destructiveness: namely, the beloved, client king. Section 4 considers a broadly similar case: the Golden Calf story, when Yhwh threatens to annihilate the chosen people. By lofting such a radical threat, Yhwh jeopardizes a character who is, in other literary contexts, unassailable: God's own people.

These texts, Psalm 89 and the Golden Calf story (Exod 32), in effect *empty* another figure of the privileges and prerogatives that they exercise in other textual configurations. Divine aggression accomplishes that evacuation, and it leaves one character as the exclusive possessor of divine safety.

As noted, these arguments function within a *textual* parameter (textual evidence simply and solely authorizes arguments about textual rhetoric). This means that they relate only indirectly to several important recent works that unfold the historical consequences of monotheism. These books identify the interconnections of monotheism with violence – the historical violence, that is, committed by human communities that adhere to monotheism. There may be causal threads and ligaments that bind the aggressive, sometimes even violent god *within* the biblical texts to the violent humans navigating history *outside* of the text. But such threads are not obvious. As Regina Schartz, author of one of these books, writes: "politics are not hardwired into theology, and the relation between monotheism and the social order is not simple."[17] Neither are these threads the subject that these other books examine. They do not allege that the aggression of the biblical god generates aggressive conduct in his human readers; that he provides an ideal for emulation. Rather, they contend that it is the exclusive *truth* claim of biblical monotheism, over against other, ostensibly false religions, that generates human violence,[18] or that it is the *scarcity* of exclusive divine favor and exclusive human loyalty that generates human violence.[19] Still, even if the argument of the present work does not bear straightforwardly on the concern of these other books, its concluding chapter teases out one possible juncture: the theological rationale behind the literary relaxation of biblical monotheizing by its tradents and inheritors.

2 World-Destroyer: Flood Stories

The present section stages a comparison of texts that narrate the most aggressive divine action of them all: the erasure through a flood of *all life* except one boatload of humans and animals. In keeping with the book's overall argument, the section seeks to elucidate the impact of monotheizing on the aggressiveness of the biblical god. As such, its attention is *theological*: in its first part, it looks again at the Mesopotamian flood stories, but not to give an overall historical account or literary interpretation. Rather, it draws up a profile of the gods involved in flooding and reestablishing the world, paying special attention to their aggressiveness. In the same way, when it turns in its second part to the

---

[17] Schwartz, *Curse of Cain*, 16. Indeed, some have argued that divine violence authorizes human abstention from violence! See, for example, Volf, "Divine Violence?"

[18] Assmann, *Price of Monotheism*, also Bettini, *In Praise of Polytheism*.

[19] Schwartz, *Curse of Cain*.

version of the Flood Story in the Book of Genesis, it focuses on the way these scriptural texts render the biblical god. Insofar as the scriptural texts concentrate various roles of the Mesopotamian flood story into *one* divine self, the section inquires: how and in what ways does that rhetorical move increase the biblical god's aggression? The basic claim, which this and following sections demonstrate, is that monotheizing amplifies divine aggression. The final part of the section considers literary contexts and counterbalances of the Genesis Flood Story.

The Mesopotamian Flood

First, then, the flood story in its ancient (pre-biblical) editions: there are three primary versions of the Mesopotamian flood story, one in Sumerian and two in Akkadian. Each is attested by several individual cuneiform copies.

- The first version is sometimes called "Eridu Genesis." The oldest and longest copy of Eridu Genesis dates to circa 1600 BCE and was written in Sumerian in the city of Nippur. The human hero in this version is named Ziusudra, a king and priest.[20]
- The second version is an epic work called "The Epic of Atrahasis," after the name of its human hero, Atrahasis; it is written in Old Babylonian and its two multi-tablet copies date to circa 2000–1600 BCE.[21]
- The most famous and widely copied of the ancient Mesopotamian versions is the third: the eleventh tablet of the Gilgamesh Epic. Although the Gilgamesh Epic is very old – originating in the third millennium BCE – the "canonical" edition that includes the flood story is found in Standard Babylonian (ca. 1000–900 BCE).[22] It identifies the flood hero by the name Utnapishtim (although the earlier name Atrahasis shows through twice).

The three Mesopotamian versions of the flood story put the disaster to various work, narratively. Eridu Genesis and the Atrahasis Epic tell a tale whose broad outlines parallel the opening eleven chapters of the Book of Genesis: they begin with the creation of humans, proceed to the flood destruction, and then provide a recreative denouement. Eridu Genesis names the four highest gods as those who "fashioned the darkheaded [people]": An, Enlil, Enki, and Ninhursaga. But it is the lattermost, the goddess of birth and fertility, also known as Nintu, whose speech Eridu Genesis directly presents; she expresses care for humans and calls them her creatures ("my humankind"). She also wishes for them to build cities

---

[20] Jacobsen, "The Eridu Genesis."
[21] Wasserman, *The Flood*, 60–103; also Lambert and Millard, *Atra-Hasis*.
[22] See George, trans., *The Epic of Gilgamesh*.

and cult-places. The Atrahasis Epic starts more conflictually and goes into greater detail: in it, a contingent of lesser gods goes on strike against the high gods, even taking direct action against Enlil, their "counsellor," surrounding his temple with tools they set on fire. In response to their agitation, the high gods, led by Enlil, deputize the mother goddess Nintu to fashion humans, with the goal of offloading labor onto them. In both Eridu Genesis and Atrahasis, it is only *after* these founding events that the flood story takes place. For both tales, *labor* issues precede the flood. By contrast, the flood in the Gilgamesh Epic stands more self-contained; it is not a climactic episode in the formation of the world but a discrete unit set within the longer story of Gilgamesh's quest for immortality. Unlike the other two versions, in the Gilgamesh Epic, the flood hero relates the story himself, in first-person voice.

All three Mesopotamian recensions share common plot points. The flooding of the world is a decree by the assembly of the gods – a joint divine decision. One of the gods, Enki, is a special patron of the human flood hero. Enki warns him ahead of time to build a boat and save his life. In Atrahasis, this warning is framed in terms of a dispute between the flood hero's guardian god, Enki, and the high god Enlil. The man Atrahasis says to the elders of his city:

> my god [Enki] came to a disagreement with your god,
> hence Enki and Enlil became steadily angry (with one another), (and) expelled me
> from my city.
> Since I lastingly revere Enki, he told me of this matter. I will not dwell in your city,
> I cannot set my feet on the earth of Enlil.[23]

After the joint decree of the gods, in all three recensions, the flood comes. The Atrahasis and Gilgamesh epics describe a veritable concerto of divine aggression. Both accounts commence with the thundering of the storm god, Adad. Two herald-gods, Shullat and Hanish, go as vanguards of the invasion, walking over the mountains and the land. More serious events of unmaking follow in their wake. Each god, responsible for some particular domain, reverses its normal function. The god of the netherworld, Errakal, pulls out the dams that stop up the primeval waters. Ninurta, responsible for irrigation, breaks the dykes. The Annukaki gods set the land itself ablaze. Adad smashes the land like a pot. The wind billows, darkness falls. Noise increases: "The Flood bellowed like a bull, like a screeching eagle the winds howled."[24]

In fact the gods set in motion a cataclysm of such scale that they become afraid and withdraw up into a higher heaven. They huddle and cower;

---

[23] Wasserman, *The Flood*, 32. Compare George, *Gilgamesh* at ibid., 115.
[24] Wassermann, *The Flood*, 34.

Gilgamesh says that "they curled up like dogs."[25] Deprived of the offerings that humans make to them in the cult, the gods are also left thirsty and hungry. They weep – whether from fear or hunger or regret, it is not clear.

After seven days and seven nights, the flood relents. The sun shines again. There is "a sudden silence."[26] The flood hero disembarks, in Gilgamesh after sending out three successive birds, and he makes offerings to the gods. Famished, the gods "grouped around the offering like flies" (a line appearing in both Atrahasis and Gilgamesh). In the longer, Akkadian versions of the story, another stage of the conflict between gods then ensues. Enlil sees the boat and is filled with rage. He exclaims: "All we great Annunaki decided together on oath! ... How did man survive the destruction?"[27] Another god, Anu in Atrahasis, Ninurta in Gilgamesh, then points to Enki: "Who but Enki could do this?" Having been called out like this, Enki, the special patron to the flood hero, responds with a counteraccusation for Enlil: "how did you bring the flood without deliberation?" and he defends his renegade action of warning the flood hero.

The divine aggression that submerges the world is, across all three versions, a matter of *activity* and not of *affect*. The decreation of the cosmos is a concerted effort, with each god making a distinctive contribution. But the gods are not described as *enraged* while doing so. They are simply carrying out the verdict they reached in council together. Divine anger – the specific emotional vocabulary of *itetezizu* and *mali*, anger and rage[28] – bookends the flood but does not drive it. And, divine anger faces not toward human beings but between the gods themselves. As noted, at least in Atrahasis, Enki and Enlil were mutually angry with each other *before* the flood. Enlil is also enraged *after* the flood, because the other gods exempted one human from the destruction they had decided as a body – but at his initiative – to prosecute.

Another affective note is relevant to divine aggression; it is unique to the Atrahasis Epic (though Eridu Genesis lacks it likely by an accident of preservation). No *reason* for the flood is given in the Gilgamesh Epic. As David Clines observes, "the causes of the Flood are not especially relevant to [its] question [about human immortality]."[29] By contrast, Atrahasis *does* supply a reason for the flood: the multiplication of humans results in noise and uproar, indeed "the land bellow[ing] like a bull." All this hubbub disturbs Enlil, the same god whose house the lower, laborer gods had surrounded; he is the god who instigated the creation of humans to take over those gods' work responsibilities.

---

[25] Wasserman, *The Flood*, 117.   [26] Wasserman, *The Flood*, 133.
[27] Wasserman, *The Flood*, 36; compare George, *Gilgamesh*, at ibid., 119.
[28] Cl I 43; Cl vi 5. See Wasserman's note in *The Flood*, 43.
[29] Clines, "Noah's Flood 1," 130.

Enlil heard their noise
And addressed the great gods
"The noise [*rigmu*] of mankind has become too intense for me,
With their uproar [*ḫubur*] I am deprived of sleep."[30]

This text would be, to refer to Matthew Schlimm's words from the previous section, a good candidate for containing "implicit anger." No terms designating anger are present; and yet the experience of losing sleep because of noise pollution irresistibly evokes irritation or frustration. This is especially so in view of the destruction of humans that follows. In her speech – on which, more later – the mother goddess points to Enlil's advocacy in seeking to annihilate humankind: "Enlil pressed and made me utter [the decree]." After the flood, she puts the decision in his mouth alone: "Enlil ... Your mouth issued a final verdict, now their [the humans'] bright faces are dark forever."[31] In her perspective, the destruction of the world traces back to Enlil, and the cause that the narrative supplies for his destructive will is sleeplessness.

Several interpretations of the human "noise" exist. A few older scholarly works understand the human din in a moral dimension: humans failed to respect the boundary between themselves and the gods.[32] Divine aggression on this telling reinforces the boundary: it is punitive and protective. In the judgment of other commentators, though, this explanation is "overly moralistic and even anachronistic, for it is too heavily influenced by the Biblical tradition."[33] Another influential interpretation posits *overpopulation* as the reason for the flood. Human noisiness indexes proliferation, and the flood is but the severest attempt by the gods to reduce humans back into a more manageable number. The ending of the Atrahasis version may support this understanding: its final stanza describes the post-flood creation of barren women, celibate female priesthoods, and infant-snatching demons – all phenomena that contribute to reducing population.[34] These non-birthing beings are, in effect, smaller-scale echoes and aftereffects of the worldwide flood. The gods' aggression finds a more modest and regularized outlet in human experience.[35]

The Mesopotamian flood story thus yields up a rich picture of divine aggression. There is a conflict, above human heads, between a god who warns the flood

---

[30] Lambert and Millard, *Atra-Hasis*, 67.　[31] Wasserman, *The Flood*, 34.
[32] Pettinato, "Die Bestrafung des Menschengeschlechts"; also Von Soden, "Der Mensch bescheidet sich nicht."
[33] Lang, "Floating from Babylon to Rome," 213.
[34] Draffkorn Kilmer, "The Mesopotamian Concept of Overpopulation."
[35] Wasserman, *The Flood*, 130–133. Wasserman advances a reading focused on *sound*. He observes that *noise* plays a key role in the rhetoric of the whole Babylonian flood story. The flood represents the "vocal climax" of the story, and total silence succeeds it. Postdiluvian human life is one marked by relative quiet and aloneness.

hero and a god whose idea it was to make humans in the first place. Self-interest haunts the motive of both gods: Enki has a sense of fairness, that each person should bear the penalty for their own conduct – but the flood hero's own speech identifies a different and more selfish incentive for the god's warning: "Since I lastingly revere Enki, he told me of this matter."[36] The reverence of the flood hero tips the scales: Enki's willingness to conflict with Enlil reflects a reciprocity between human client and divine patron. So, too, Enlil's inspiration to make humans comes from the work stoppage of the lower gods. His vexation because of their noise causes him to call for their destruction. For neither god is the matter of destroying humans (or saving humans) a dispassionate affair.

The conflict between these two gods lends the divine aggression a dramatic quality: one god objects to the fate of humans and takes secret, vigilante action to preserve life, while the other god uses his powerful position to convince the council of gods to act destructively to relieve his own personal discomfort. The booming and cracking of the flood itself, and the terror of the gods, gives the aggression an awesome scale. The flood is a juggernaut: it exceeds even the gods' own intentions. It frightens even its creators.

But there is one other affective note that colors the aggression of the flood story: regret. One goddess in particular embodies grief and self-recrimination as well as memory. Nintu is the "birth-goddess and the creatress of [hu]mankind."[37] From out of clay mixed with the flesh and blood of a slain god, and with a powerful incantation, she fashioned humans. In the midst of the flood event, she weeps and wails over their annihilation. She expresses incomprehension, and she blames the instigation of Enlil. Perhaps most intriguingly, she articulates a sense of incoherency with herself: she acted out of sync with herself. The aggression that issued from her shared decision with the rest of the gods was, at some deep level, inconsistent with her care for humankind. She says:

> In the assembly of the gods, how did I, with them, render the annihilation?
> Enlil pressed and made me utter it: like that Tiruru, he confused my words.
> Contrary to my own nature, against my very self, I have listened to Enlil's
>   command regarding their [the people's] noise.
> It is my blame that my offspring have become like flies![38]

After the flood, when the gods have gathered ("like flies") to Atrahasis's offering, the goddess Nintu raises her voice once more. She inveighs against the highest god Anu's abdication of responsibility and against Enlil's reckless-ness. She also says that "wailing is [my] destiny." Her grief will endure, and to ensure that she remembers the flood, she fashions flies into a necklace: "let these

---

[36] Wasserman, *The Flood*, 32.   [37] Lambert and Millard, *Atra-Hasis*, 57.
[38] Wasserman, *The Flood*, 34; also ibid., 140–145.

flies be the lapis lazuli around my neck, that I may remember these days."[39] Wasserman notes that "flies form a central image in the Flood: the dead look like flies, the gods gather around the offering like flies, and the mother-goddess wears a necklace made of (golden) flies, a *symbolon* serving to remind her of the horrors of the flood."[40]

In sum, an event of massive, frightful divine destructiveness lies at the center of the Mesopotamian flood myth: the gods by joint decision undo creation. But that aggression is surrounded on all sides by other instances of divine aggression, which are rendered in far more affective terms. The gods' verdict in council arises from the agitation of one god, Enlil, whose sleep is interrupted by human noise; his experience could well count as "implicit anger." In one version, his upset finds a mirror image in the upset of another god, Enki: "Enki and Enlil became steadily angry with one another." If on one side, the mutual anger of gods contextualizes the flood event, other examples of divine anger follow it on the far side. Enlil is enraged at Enki's action of sparing the flood hero; and, poignantly, the mother goddess is angry at Enlil – aggrieved at the loss of humans that she made – and angry at herself. She resolves to memorialize this event, by fashioning a memento.

The Biblical Flood

The biblical Flood Story takes place across four chapters (Gen 6–9) early on in the Book of Genesis. As with the Mesopotamian Eridu Genesis and Atrahasis Epic, Genesis embeds the flood within a larger account of how the world assumed its current-day shape. Across all three of these literary works, the deluvial destruction of (almost) all humankind closely follows the creation of humans. In the Bible, Yhwh God expels the first human couple from the garden as a preventative measure, lest they take from the tree of life and so become immortal, and hence even more godlike than discerning between good and evil already made them (3:22).[41] The following chapter 4 narrates the first fratricide. The guilty party Cain goes on to found a city and to father a lineage responsible for music and metallurgy (Gen 4:17–22). These developments are ambiguous – knowing good and evil is elsewhere commended (Solomon in 1 Kgs 3:9–10), and Hebrew Scripture is hardly uniform in its opposition to urban existence.[42] But they are developments, moving the story forward toward a world more like our own. The flood intervenes just here.

---

[39] Wasserman, *The Flood*, 35.   [40] Wasserman, *The Flood*, 56.

[41] Genesis 2-3 use the compound divine name "Yhwh *elohim*," here translated Yhwh God, twenty times in total. Outside of these chapters it appears only a few times in Chronicles and Psalms.

[42] See Blum, "Urgeschichte."

The biblical version shares plot elements with its Mesopotamian antecedents.[43] As with Atrahasis, it is concerned with human labor: the notice of Noah's birth includes a prayer, or perhaps a prophecy, by his father, Lamech: "he named him Noah, saying, 'Out of the ground that Yhwh has cursed, this one shall bring us relief from our work and from the toil of our hands'" (Gen 5:29). The verb for "relief," √*nwḥ*, sounds like Noah, so that one might paraphrase the promise about bringing relief as: "he will *noah* us." Noah's destiny is to undo the difficulty of human work ensuing from God's curse on the first human couple: "cursed is the ground because of you; in toil you shall eat of it" (Gen 3:17b). There is a transposition here: in the Old Babylonian story, humans are made to toil as substitutes for the lesser, worker gods. A labor dispute precedes human existence, and humans inherit it. In the Hebrew story, work itself predates the conflict between humans and God; God made the first human to till and keep the earth, while the unpleasant hardship of work derives from a conflict that humans themselves generate. The point is: humans have absorbed the suffering role of the Mesopotamian under-gods, the Igigi. The Bible also pins a proto-messianic hope on one human, Noah. Humans play an aggrandized role relative to their Mesopotamian counterparts.

The Genesis Flood Story also resembles Atrahasis in that it draws human multiplication into its literary orbit. The text directly before the biblical Flood Story begins with human increase: "when the people began to multiply on the face of the ground . . . " (Gen 6:1). And that story features a divine pronounce-ment by which Yhwh sets a limit on the human lifespan: "My spirit shall not abide in mortals forever, for they are flesh; their days shall be one hundred twenty years" (6:3). Yhwh accomplishes by fiat, a spoken word, what the high god Enlil sought to do by sending wasting disease on humankind and by producing famine through withholding rain. Yhwh controls human increase by establishing a ceiling for the individual person, whereas Enlil controls human increase through more scattershot, and crueler, strategies. Either way, a plenitude of humans precedes the worldwide destruction.

The divine motivations for accomplishing such immense destruction diverge significantly. Even though human increase is prelude to the flood in both Mesopotamian and biblical accounts, the Bible contains no direct parallel to Enlil's annoyance at human noise. Instead, the literary environment of the biblical flood suggests a certain divine *protectiveness* as motive. Yhwh's incen-tive for capping the human lifespan is obscure; Genesis links the multiplication of humans to the incursion of "sons of *elohim*," also called Nephilim, who

---

[43] On the probable literary relationship of the biblical Flood Story to the Mesopotamian versions, see Carr, *Formation of Genesis*, 141–177; Day, "Comparative Ancient Near Eastern Study."

intermarry with human women (Gen 6:2a, 4a). Their children are "the heroes that were of old, warriors of renown" (6:4b). Genesis does not specify what divine affect, if any, this intermixing of beings and their powerful offspring elicits. But in context of Yhwh God's express prior concern to reserve immortality to the divine world – what Lee Humphreys identifies as divine *jealousy*[44] – it is easy to read the Nephilim episode in the same emotional key. The emergence of mighty, hybrid warriors presented a threat to Yhwh God's exclusive divine power, just as continued human presence in the garden threatened his exclusive divine immortality. In both cases, Yhwh acts to safeguard divine privilege.

The presence of a certain protectiveness makes the biblical god ambivalent as a character. This is, after all, the same god who blessed humans and commanded them to multiply. Now they *have* multiplied on the face of the earth, but in a fashion that apparently endows their descendants with too much power, and Yhwh acts to handicap them. As such, the fixing of a limit to human longevity is only one in a series of episodes where Yhwh appears to act over against his own prior intention. He authorized the first humans to eat from any tree except the tree of the knowledge of good and evil, but then he changes his mind about the humans eating from another tree, the tree of life. Or again: Yhwh exiled the first humans from the garden, but then clothed them with animal skins. He exiled Cain, but he also protects him. Jack Miles comments provocatively: "As a character, the Lord God is disturbing as anyone is disturbing who holds immense power and seems not to know what he wants to do with it."[45]

What is important about Yhwh's ambivalence for the present book is this: such complicated motives arise from *monotheizing*. In the Mesopotamian stories, the fault lines of dramatic conflict run between gods. Rivalry and recrimination occur between them, and humans are relatively passive. Even when human increase presents a problem, it is a displacement of an intra-divine labor issue. Genesis, however, foregrounds conflict between the god Yhwh and humans. No rivalry or recrimination obtains on the "divine side" of the boundary in the Bible. This is not possible – at least not overtly – when the divine realm literally contains but one salient god. (There are multiple *elohim,* "divine beings," in Genesis, but not in such a way that any individual gods act over against Yhwh.) The dramatic action must therefore happen between that one god and another, nondivine agency – humans. Both "parts" are thereby amplified: humans are more active and significant, and Yhwh/God is more ambivalent.[46] Protectiveness, even jealousy, is the literary precipitate of configuring one god as supreme.

---

[44] Humphreys, *The Character of God,* 51.   [45] Miles, *God,* 35.
[46] This section refers to "Yhwh/God" with a slash because the biblical Flood Story is a composite of two sources and it alternates between these two divine names (Day, "Comparative Ancient Near Eastern Study").

Even if protectiveness is not the chief motive for divine destruction through the flood, its significance in the background of Genesis shows a distinct recalibration of concerns relative to the Mesopotamian recensions. The Mesopotamian stories lack this affect entirely; the gods are not policing their prerogatives over against humans. Divine protectiveness in Genesis on the other hand emboldens the human-divine border, makes it axial. Humans who transgress the boundary are rebuffed: expelled from the garden, limited in their lifespan, scattered away from their tower. But alongside protectiveness, another divine motive far more directly drives the flooding of the world in Genesis: grief and regret.

The notice about the Nephilim segues into the Flood Story proper. The word for humankind – Hebrew *adam* – runs like connective tissue through the text: the *adam* began to multiply (6:1), the sons of *elohim* saw the daughters of the *adam* (6:2a, cf. 6:4), Yhwh says his spirit will not dwell in the *adam* (6:3). And, in verse 5, Yhwh saw the evildoing of the *adam*, that it was great. Indeed, Yhwh's gaze pierces to the human interior: "every form of their heart's planning was only evil all the day."[47] In its literary context, the only evildoing is the hybridizing of divine beings with human women. But this does not seem to match the extremity of Yhwh's observation. Surely not every intention in the depths of the human heart went toward intermarrying with sons of god. A different and more radical problem lies open to Yhwh's perception.

A subsequent verse frames the issue from a different vantage, not of evildoing in general but of unmaking. Genesis 6:11 reads: "the earth was corrupt before the *elohim*; the earth was full of violence." The key Hebrew words in these successive clauses suggest ruination and aggression. Their reference is vague. In what ways might humans, or all creatures, participate in corroding the earth and saturating it with violence? Here the creation stories provide a necessary setup to the flood narrative: there, in the opening chapters of Genesis, God creates all things, separating each from the chaos waters, setting it in its own integrity, tasking it with specific activity. Here at the outset of the Flood Story, Yhwh/God notices that the beings he fashioned are swerving from their appointed pathways. They are undermining their integrity – through murder, in the Cain story, and in Lamech his violent descendant; through intermixing with the Nephilim. They are unmaking themselves. The biblical god beholds that his creation is decreating itself.

As the creator, abhorrence or even anger might be the divine affect we infer from this spectacle of creation corrupting and violating itself. But in fact the symmetry between the maker god and unmaking humanity sets the conditions for a quite different divine emotion. The Common English Bible (CEB) translates Gen 6:6 as follows: "The Lord regretted making human beings on the earth, and

---

[47] Fox, *The Five Books of Moses*, 33.

he was heartbroken." The first verb (Hebrew: √*nḥm*) translated as *regretted* primarily describes a decision, a change of mind, more than a *feeling* of remorse or loss. Older English versions translate with *repent*: Yhwh repented. The same verb sometimes features a human subject. The prophet Jeremiah puts these words, for example, in the mouth of Ephraim:

> After I strayed,
>   I repented [√*nḥm*];
> after I came to understand,
>   I beat my breast.
> I was ashamed and humiliated
>   because I bore the disgrace of my youth (31:9).

More frequently, however, the Hebrew Bible ascribes the activity of *repenting* to a divine subject, or it threatens that God will *not* repent (change his mind) with regard to a threatened act of destruction. That said, Gen 6:6 supplies the first biblical example of divine repenting.[48] Notice, too, that in Gen 6:6, God's change of mind concerns the initial act of creating humans, rather than God's resolve to destroy them through the flood. God rues making humans in the first place. It is arguably the Bible's saddest verse.

The second verb of Gen 6:6 (√ʿṣb) is more clearly affective: Yhwh was *heartbroken*, according to the CEB rendering. More literally: "Yhwh grieves himself – to his heart" (Literal Standard Version). The next occurrence of this word for *grieving* in the Book of Genesis is Gen 34:7, when it articulates the reaction of Jacob's sons to the rape of their sister Dina. There it is paired with a phrase for anger: "the men were grieved [√ʿṣb] and very angry, because [Shechem] had done a disgraceful thing in Israel" (NKJV).[49] Nowhere else in the Bible is this verb for grieving brought together with the Hebrew phrase that follows, *to his heart*.[50] Humphreys writes: "the fruits of human hearts bring an ache to Yahweh's heart."[51]

Yhwh's decision to flood the world issues from out of this regret and heart-brokenness. His reaction to creation's unmaking of itself is not abhorrence or anger, but rather, regret and emotional pain. Importantly, the story does not show Yhwh lashing out; nor acting retributively, visiting an extrinsic or punitive sentence on wicked humanity. Rather, Yhwh sees the derangement of the world through corruption and violence, and then Yhwh in effect *completes* that derangement. Humans are pulling out the threads; Yhwh rips out the seams.

---

[48] On this topic, see especially Sonnet, "God's Repentance."

[49] See Humphreys, *The Character of God*, 263 n. 7.

[50] Though see Gen 8:21, where the latter phrase occurs again: "Yhwh smelled the sweet savor; and Yhwh said to His heart . . . ."

[51] Humphreys, *The Character of God*, 65.

The Flood Story plays out as a point by point account of decreation. The waters of the deep below that God had contained, he releases (Gen 6:11). He opens the windows of heaven such that the waters above the firmament tumble down (6:11). Creation collapses back into its original state of watery chaos.

Relative to the divine aggression at the center of the Mesopotamian versions of the flood story, the biblical account evidences several transformations. At one level, it is true that these texts *monotheize*: they concentrate all the divine powers onto a singular divine character, Yhwh/God, with the result that he plays all the various parts. He is at once the instigator of the flood and its executor. He is the restorer of the created order after the flood waters ebb. He is, in the end, *more destructive* than any individual divine counterpart within the Mesopotamian stories; as a single character he performs the destructive work that a concerto of gods accomplished. This amply warrants the Element's main argument: monotheizing amplifies aggression. At the same time, however, Yhwh is the one who grieves, whose heart aches because of human evil. In its monotheizing, Hebrew Scripture makes Yhwh take on the affective part of the mother goddess. Indeed, the biblical version *foregrounds* this aspect of the divine persona: instead of having the goddess weep *after* the flood is over and done, the Book of Genesis places divine grief and regret *before* the flood destruction, in response to the violence of humankind. Besides protectiveness of divine privilege, these painful emotions are the primary divine motive for plunging the world back into water.

Literarily importing the mother goddess Nintu into Yhwh suggests a kind of resolution to his characterological ambivalence. She alone from among the Mesopotamian gods voices a sense of incoherency with herself: she acted, in her words, "contrary to my own nature, against my very self." She made humans, painstakingly, with handcrafting and magical words. She cannot understand how she then consented to their destruction. The biblical text likewise holds a tension, as noted, between Yhwh/God's creatorship and his willful diminishment of human capacities: he makes and blesses but he also expels and handicaps. More than that, in the flood, he undoes and submerges. The Book of Genesis puts divine grief and heartsickness at the literary hinge point between these competing divine dynamics. The text *narrates* rival directions of the divine will; and when it gives a glimpse into the divine psyche that holds such duality, it yields up a picture of *pain*. In this regard, it appropriates and aggrandizes the mother goddess. This should be seen as a reflex of its monotheizing. *Because* it monotheizes, it relocates conflict either between humans and God or within God's own self. It therefore plays up the part of the self-conflicted mother goddess. Nintu gives the biblical writer(s) a template for the grief-stricken, decreating creator.

This textual reallocation, of the regretful mother goddess into Yhwh/God, bespeaks another literary effect of monotheizing. As noted, humans are more active and significant in the biblical story than the Mesopotamian, because conflict within the "divine world" is unavailable to the latter as a narrative resource. Hence, in the biblical Flood Story, it is not that Yhwh plays *all* the destructive parts. The text does not show him breaking the dykes, setting the land ablaze, smashing the earth like a pot. Rather, his activities are subtler, almost behind the scenes. They are, in a word, *completive*: they exaggerate and bring to full force the disintegration that humans have already put in motion. Instead of the sleep-deprived Enlil, *humans* in some sense play the initiatory role in the biblical version of the worldwide flood. Even so, Yhwh takes sole responsibility for the disaster: "I am about to bring the Flood" (Gen 6:17).

Yhwh also promises after the flood never to repeat this world-destroying action. These verses reiterate his exclusive responsibility; they showcase his destructive power. He commits himself as a solo entity to forego what the Mesopotamian gods achieved as a council. But the scenes of Yhwh God after the flood also and in particular extend the literary appropriation of the goddess Nintu. The Atrahasis Epic depicts her after the flood, making a memento out of flies, as a grisly reminder to her of the loss of the humans she made. Like her, Yhwh memorializes the flood destruction. He sets a bow in the heavens "as a sign between Me and You and every living creature with you, for all ages to come" (Gen 9:12). Although it is visible to all creatures in the sky, the bow in fact faces toward God himself. Its function is to remind *him* of his renunciation: "when the bow is in the clouds, I will see it and remember the everlasting covenant between God and all living creatures" (9:16; cf. 9:14–15).

There is, once more, transposition: flies in the Atrahasis story are the result of mass death, whereas the bow is the instrument of mass death. The goddess Nintu places the necklace of flies on her own person, like lapis lazuli; the biblical god places the bow out of his own reach, into the heavenlies. But the literary adaptation still attests the intensive way that Genesis reworks the mother goddess character into Yhwh: he shares her conflicted, pained experience. He, like her, wishes never to forget this event, perhaps even to learn from it, to make his subsequent divine career different because of it. Within the biblical retelling of the flood, her character is the most intact; there is most resemblance between the biblical god and her. By piecing out her post-flood grief to Yhwh *before* the flood, the Book of Genesis holds Yhwh's creatorship and destructiveness in an acute literary tension; by keeping and repurposing her commemoration *after* the flood, Genesis ensures that the whole episode is decisive for Yhwh's character, too.

Conclusion: Literary Contexts and Counterbalances

Is the biblical god more aggressive than his Mesopotamian counterparts? The answer is yes: they unmake the world as a team effort. He goes it alone, and the Bible's presentation of his aggression follows from its literary strategy of *monotheizing*. Hebrew Scripture concentrates all divine powers into this one divine person. As previous sections indicate, this aggregation has some follow-on effects: because the scriptural text treats one god as the primary, relevant deity, it cannot afford to show open, dramatic conflict between multiple gods. It thus must literarily gerrymander conflict between gods onto the human-divine boundary. This elevates the role of humans relative to God. Some conflict, however, it relocates within the single divine person, and as such, it must draw on some theological resource that can give coherence to a complex divine personality, a god at once creative and destructive. It appears that Genesis finds this resource in Nintu: it models Yhwh's character most on the grieving, self-conflicted mother goddess.[52] More than irritated Enlil, more than renegade Enki, more than the various gods that wreak destruction on the earth, Yhwh appears, like she does, hurt, heartsick, regretful. His aggression emerges from these affective taproots. But this technique, too, results from monotheizing: it is a characterological way of resolving the tensions that arise from concentrating several competing divine roles into the same single divine being. Genesis "Nintuizes" because it monotheizes.

Even so, the people responsible for transmitting the biblical Flood Story sought in numerous ways to contextualize and reinterpret it. By placing it in the so-called Genesis Prologue, early readers of the story gave it a foundational significance: the Flood Story helps to explain how the world came to be in its current shape. By the same token, however, the flood belongs to a primordial time, which is different from the present. The flood has an *ephapax* significance: a once-and-for-all completeness; an unrepeatability. God himself, as observed, pledges never to flood the world again. Unlike with many other biblically narrated events, generations of Jewish and Christian readers did not find the Flood Story interesting because it was iterable or paradigmatic. Rather, it is unique, decisive, always in the past. Thus one literary context: in its canonical configuration, the Flood Story is set permanently into the long ago and far away.

Besides this contextualization to the primeval past, Jewish and Christian readers also engaged the Flood Story in less monotheizing forms. As Section 1 indicates, the Hebrew Bible's monotheizing approach did not persuade all the inheritors of its traditions. Some recipients of the flood story therefore *disaggregated* what the Genesis text puts together. They de-monotheized. The Book of the Watchers from within 1 Enoch provides a case study in just such relaxation of the

---

[52] Compare Keel, "Yahweh as Mother Goddess."

biblical concentration of all divine powers into one god.[53] Dating to the third century BCE, this work may reflect a stratum of the flood story that predates the Genesis version: the biblical text may epitomize Enoch materials.[54] Watchers is far more like the Mesopotamian editions than it is like the Genesis one, at least insofar as conflict occurs *between* divine beings and not only along the divine-human line; and the psyche of the biblical god is no longer the painful site of regret and grief, the home of conflicting impulses.

In the Book of the Watchers, the problem that precipitates the flood is not human noise, nor is it human violence. It is the rebellious angels. Two hundred of them swear an oath together; the evil they perpetrate is multiform: "they took wives from among [humans] such as they chose. And they began to go into them, and to defile themselves through them, and to teach them sorcery and charms, and to reveal to them the cutting of roots and plants" (1 En 7:1). Notably, it is not God who initiates a response to their wickedness; instead it is four archangels, Michael and Sariel and Raphael and Gabriel, who look down from heaven and see bloodshed and godlessness and violence (9:1). They heed the cries of the earth and the petitions of the holy ones of heaven, "the souls of men" (9:3). They approach the Lord of Ages and report to him what is happening, and the Most High then sends them out, each with a task: warning Noah, imprisoning one of the angels, destroying the hybrid children of the angels, and destroying all perversity from the face of the earth (10:16).

In short, divine destructiveness is *delegated* to these archangels. The Most High gives a command, but these angelic beings are its executors. No longer is Yhwh the one personally opening the floodgates of heaven. Nor does Enoch provide any window into Yhwh's psyche; there is no hint of a troubled or pained inner divine self. The Book of the Watchers has no need to resolve conflicting divine intentions: it makes no use of the Nintu persona, because the divine roles of registering a cosmic problem and warning the flood hero and cleansing the world are distributed back to several distinct divine characters. God is left in a high and supervisory place. Watchers is monotheistic in the sense that he is clearly the sovereign; the angels serve at his command. But God is characterologically far smaller, flatter, and remote. The monotheizing strategy of Genesis is, in comparison, much more integral and thoroughgoing. It yields a more conflicted and aggressive divine character. It is unclear if devotion or repugnance, or simply a change of intellectual eras, generated the popularity of Enoch relative to Genesis for several centuries of Jewish and Christian reading. But the point remains: the recipients of the monotheizing biblical flood account worked

---

[53] Nickelsburg and VanderKam, *1 Enoch*.
[54] See Milik, *Books of Enoch*; also Davies, "And Enoch Was Not."

to contain it, by situating it literarily into the past, and also by telling a much more angelically populated version of it.

3 Regicide: Royal Texts

The present section considers divine aggression from a different angle than the preceding section. It does not compare two instances of textualized aggression, one from the ancient world and the other from Hebrew Scripture, in order to argue that Hebrew texts aggregate divine powers that are distributed elsewhere, with the result of intensifying the aggressiveness of the biblical god. Rather, the present section examines one set of ancient texts that *wholly exempt* a certain figure – the king – from the destructive power of the patron god; and it then shows how several biblical texts close that exemption. They subject the king to God's aggression. In so doing, the present section argues that these scriptural texts *monotheize* by concentrating divine power into a single character. Unlike the previous section, that concentration has an *evacuative* rather than *aggregative* force. Textually treating one god alone as god *takes away* in addition to *adding up*; placing all the divine power and privilege into one divine character removes it from another character – the human king. In its conclusion, the section looks to the literary contexts and counterbalances within which subsequent Jewish and Christian readers interpreted the figure of God's beloved king.

Royal Inscriptions

But first it must be shown that some human characters in ancient texts enjoy a protected status relative to other human characters in virtue of their participation in divinity. More specifically, some inscriptions commissioned by kings depict those kings as sons of the principal national gods. This divine sonship serves various rhetorical purposes. Divine sonship reassures of the king's legitimacy (oftentimes fictitiously, in the case of usurpers): the firstborn of the patron god has all possible claim to the throne, even if the previous king was not their father! Divine sonship evokes the mutual devotion of god and king; and a beloved and pious king is a good king, deserving of loyalty from the populace.[55] But perhaps most pressingly, in the rhetorical program of royal inscriptions, divine sonship shelters the king from the gods' destructive power. And this destructive power is the crescendo of such inscriptions.

All these dynamics can be seen from one representative inscription, Tel Ahmar 6 (the Ahmar/Qubbah stele).[56] The latter is written in Luwian, an Indo-European language within the Anatolian family of languages. A king named

---

[55] See Thompson, "A Testimony of the Good King."　　[56] Payne, *Luwian Inscriptions*, 93–94.

Hamiyatas, ruler of the land Masuwari, commissioned it around 900 BCE. He introduces himself like so, in first-person voice:

"I am the ruler of Hamiyatas, king of Masuwari, servant of the Storm God" (§1).

Of first importance, he lines out his relationship to the gods:

And they loved me, the firstborn child: the heavenly Storm God, Ea, the Grain God, the Moon God, the affectionate Sun God, Runtiya, Karhuha, Kubaba, Hepat, and Šauška of the Army, Teššub, Šarruma, Heaven and Earth, the Gods [. . . broken] the ANDA TASAMINZI Gods. And they granted me my paternal succession (§§2–3).

The gods are manifold, though the Storm God is first in sequence. Their basic posture toward Hamiyatas is love; they *loved* him, and indeed, he is their firstborn child. The first concrete result of that divine love and that divine sonship is *succession*. The rest of the inscription lays out a more detailed history of how Hamiyatas assumed the throne and exercised rule. This history appeals to two audiences, human and divine. It serves the dual purpose of commending the Good King to the text's human readership; and it commends the king to the divine community, since it spells out his fealty to them (and their past aid lent to him). Tel Ahmar 6 features topoi that are typical of royal inscriptions: the king's achievements face outward toward enemies of the realm and inward toward temple renovations and public works.[57] On both counts, the king demonstrates his fitness for continued support from both human subjects and superhuman patrons.

Hamiyatas thus tells of his military prowess: he destroyed the enemies of Masuwari. Notably, he did this "with the help of my Lord" (§4–7). Twice he insists that "the Storm God of the Army ran before me." The patron god fought in the vanguard of his army, wreaking destruction on behalf of his beloved king. To any human readers of the inscription, this past example presents an implicit warning: gods, even the Storm God, go to battle for Hamiyatas. He is not to be opposed. To any divine readers of the inscription, the Storm God's intervention in war presents a precedent and perhaps a prayer along the lines of a biblical psalm: you acted like this before – so act like this again.

Hamiyatas also tells of his devotion to the gods. He says that he "provided the way for the gods, and I established a full ritual for them" (§12). Later he provides a more specific memory: "One belonging to the god [presumably a prophet] spoke to me: Cause the Storm God of the Army to dwell here" (§22). Hamiyatas answers this prophetic commandment with compliance: "in that year I settled the Storm God of the Army . . . and I shall always give nine

---

[57] See Green, "*I Undertook Great Works*"; also Suriano, "The Apology of Hazael."

oxen to this Storm God of the Army." These lines recollect Hamiyatas's establishment of a temple site and his "settling" of the Storm God, probably in the form of a cult statue. They record his commitment to maintaining that particular site as well. Such devotion curries divine favor; as such, it engenders human loyalty, because human citizens of Masuwari want to get in on the divine goodwill that Hamiyatas accrues.

But the crescendo of the inscription happens in its final lines. There its dual audience comes most clearly into focus; the message it telegraphs throughout reaches a level of directness. Above all, the inscription is concerned to uphold the name and legacy of Hamiyatas the king. It threatens any would-be human vandals; and it appeals via a curse-prayer to the patron god. "Whosoever shall delete the name of Hamiyatas, or who desires evil for the descendants of Hamiyatas, for him may this Storm God of the Army become a lion! May he swallow down his head, his wife, and child!" (§§29–34).

If the body of the inscription narrates previous episodes of divine aggression, wielded against enemies of the nation, the closing curse brings that aggression prospectively into the present; and it earmarks the god's lion-like fury for a far more encompassing target. Anyone, even a citizen of Masuwari, can opt into the destructive power of the god, if only they etch out king Hamiyatas's name or purpose ill for his dynasty.

The Tel Ahmar 6 inscription says nothing about divine *affect*; neither in its account of his past devastations against Masuwari's enemies nor in the final curse does it mention the Storm God's emotions. There is no fury, wrath, or indignation. Instead, the text offers a repertoire of words communicating destructive divine activities: running ahead of the army, becoming a lion, swallowing up the head. It is for this reason the present Element frames its argument in terms of *divine aggression*: harms committed by gods against humans.

The rhetoric of Tel Ahmar 6 (and so many royal inscriptions like it) positions Hamiyatas at the furthest pole *away* from such aggression. He is loved by gods, born to the gods, militarily aided by the Storm God and exerting himself in piety for the Storm God. The closing curse wishes for divine vengeance if even his name is harmed! By contrast, the text puts this anyone ("whosoever") in nearest danger of divine aggression. They can trigger it exactly by threatening Hamiyatas. The unthinkable thought for such a text is the aggression of the patron god against the beloved king. He is exempted.

Another, similar inscription showcases the radicality of the king's exemption from divine destruction. The Hadad Inscription (KAI 214) covers the lower body of a human-shaped stone stele dating to the eighth century BCE; it is

written in Sam'alian, an Aramaic dialect.[58] Like Tel Ahmar 6, the Hadad
Inscription begins with a self-introduction. Characteristically of Northwest
Semitic inscriptions, it does not frame the king's relationship to the gods in
terms of *love*; nor does *sonship* overtly describe the king's status. Much the
same logic applies, however: the king named Pannamuwa says that "the gods
Hadad and El and Resheph and Rakkab-el and Shamash stood with me . . . and
gave into my hands a scepter of dominion" (ll. 2–3). Their sponsorship lies
behind his accession; and the text enumerates his accomplishments in war and
construction. Like Hamiyatas, king Pannamuwa reminds his divine readership
of his past devotion and their reciprocal past favor: "in the days of my dominion,
gifts were given to the gods and they indeed took them from my hands.
Whatever I asked from the gods, they indeed gave to me. And the gods were
indeed pleased with me" (l. 12).

But Pannamuwa is far more verbose in cursing than Hamiyatas – also in
blessing. The final section of the inscription first prays a blessing on
Pannamuwa's sons, conditional on their performance of certain rituals honoring
their dead father. "Now if ever any of my sons takes the scepter, and he sits on
my throne and maintains power and sacrifices to this Hadad . . . and he calls on
the name of Hadad, then he should say: May the soul of Pannamuwa eat with
you, and may the soul of Pannamuwa drink with you" (ll. 15–17). In this
possible future of blessing, Pannamuwa's soul or *nefeš* communes with the
patron god. All is well, so long as the son complies with the "ask" that the
inscription's rhetoric makes of him.

But Pannamuwa, secondly, imagines a negative possible future. Once more,
these sentences comprise the crescendo of the inscription, where its divine and
human addressees, and what it wants from each of them, is most explicit.
Pannamuwa requests his son to care for his soul; he requests of Hadad to
harm his son, should the son fall delinquent in his filial responsibility.

> If any of my sons should take the scepter and sit upon my throne as king . . . and
> not call on the name of Pannamuwa, saying: May the soul of Pannamuwa eat
> with Hadad and the soul of Pannamuwa drink with Hadad . . . with wrath may
> Hadad confound him, may he not give to him to eat because of rage and sleep
> may he withhold from him at night, but terror may he give to him (ll. 20–24).

In this scenario, divine aggression breaks out against the king's own son.
Possibly the divinely wrought harm extends even to death: some scholars
interpret a word in line 24 of the inscription as "may he put to death," that is:
may Hadad put the noncompliant son to death.[59] But even if that reading is

---

[58] Translation and discussion depend on Cornell, *Divine Aggression*, 68–78.
[59] *COS* 2:157; *TSSI* 2:61. But compare Tropper, *Inschriften*, 80.

incorrect, still Pannamuwa's curse is dire. The aggression affects the son's most basic functions of eating and sleeping and afflicts him with terror.

The fact that *even the king's son* is susceptible to injury at the hands of the patron god underlines the absoluteness of the king's exemption. The Hadad Inscription puts even the most cherished kindred to the king, his successor, in harm's way. In an even more exaggerated way than Tel Ahmar 6, the unthinkable thought in the Hadad Inscription is divine aggression against king Pannamuwa. The king is not here the beloved son exactly or directly. But still, the rhetoric of the text makes him alone the truly unconditional beneficiary of the gods.

Royal Psalms

Several biblical psalms center on a kingly figure.[60] Scholars identify such psalms as "royal psalms"; in many regards, their conceptual world maps closely onto that of royal inscriptions. They configure the king as a divine son. They describe his military prowess, authorized and empowered by the patron god; they emphasize his fealty. Crucially, they exempt the king from divine aggression, which is, as it is in inscriptions, the lynchpin and crescendo of their rhetoric.

Many differences obtain. Most noticeable is the anonymity of many royal biblical psalms: they give no name to their kingly character.[61] Royal inscriptions repeatedly call attention to the name of the king; their curse sections zero in on the possibility of the name's erasure. By leaving out the king's name, biblical psalms make the king's legacy available to others besides the king. This is in keeping with their profile as community texts. Only an individual king can "pray" the inscription, appealing to the god's past help and his own past fealty for motivation; but biblical psalms can be prayed by whomever.

A complementary characteristic of royal biblical psalms is their voice: they are not exclusively first-person and singular. In royal inscriptions, kings speak in their own voice, introducing themselves. In biblical psalms, a community or "choral" voice appears. Even in psalms when the king does speak in first-person voice, a third party bookends it. This literary device brings the psalm away from an individual kingly persona, away from the royal court, and it makes the psalm usable to a nonroyal community.[62]

Biblical psalms are also fundamentally *textual*. Unlike inscriptions that are engraved into a monument, they say nothing about their medium. They lack the

---

[60] See Cornell, "The Royal Psalms."   [61] See again Chapman, *Law and the Prophets*, 99–104.

[62] For one account of how biblical traditions might have progressed from the royal court to a nonroyal public, see Cornell, "The Value of Egyptian Aramaic" and Starbuck, "Theological Anthropology."

"this" that the previous examples feature: "this Hadad" (as in: this statue); "this Storm God of the Army." So, too, the king's success is not indexed to construction projects. The patron god does go to war on the king's behalf; and the king's reign is associated at times with particular places such as Zion. But neither the king nor the "choral voice" mentions specific temple construction projects or other public works. The royal psalms are disinvested from physical monuments.[63]

Psalm 2 exemplifies these aforementioned characteristics. It starts not with the king's voice, but that of an unnamed community, posing itself an indignant question:

> Why do nations gather | and peoples scheme vanity?
> Kings of earth make a stand | and leaders take counsel together
> against Yhwh and against his anointed one?

Indeed, there is a mimicry or recumbence: the enemy kings mutter and take counsel – but what the psalm text itself provides is a transcript of a kind of muttering and taking counsel among a different nation and people: the (implicit) nation and people aligned with Yhwh and his anointed. Still, they give no name to this anointed one.

The next verses indicate Yhwh's angry response to this conspiracy of enemy kings. As in the inscriptions, divine aggression looks initially outward, toward opponents of the home nation. Yhwh's reaction is strongly affective: "he spoke to them in his anger | in his wrath he disinherited them."[64] It is also, interestingly, verbal: Yhwh does not run ahead of the armies of the anointed; he does not give terror. He *speaks*. Psalm 2 gives the content of Yhwh's speech: "Now I myself published my king on Zion | on the mountain of my sanctuary, let me announce the decree of God."

Only then does the psalm embed the king's own first-person voice: "Yhwh said to me, 'You are my son | Today I have begotten you.'" As in Tel Ahmar 6, this divine sonship expresses the utmost value of the king to the god. It also shelters the king from the god's destructive power, which the psalm brings to the forefront in its finale. The next verses articulate divine promises made to the son: Yhwh authorizes him to break nations with an iron rod and to shatter them like vessels of a potter. More than that: the psalm's closing stanza returns to the voice of the community, and it speaks a warning about divine aggression directly to the enemy kings:

---

[63] Although compare Psalm 89 and *miqdešê*, sanctuaries, within Book III of the Psalter, which following paragraphs examine. Yet even as they grieve and protest temple destruction, these and other biblical psalms do not make the built environment integral to their rhetoric in the same way as inscriptions (see Cornell, *Divine Aggression*, 33).

[64] Following Lam, "Psalm 2 and the Disinheritance."

Serve Yhwh with fear | and rejoice with trembling
Submit sincerely, lest he be angry and you perish from the path
For his anger burns in a moment.

As with the royal inscriptions, the end of the psalm is clear about what it wants from the enemy kings: submission to Yhwh. This is quite a different action from the inscriptions, which wish for the client king's name to be unharmed (Tel Ahmar 6) or the king's *nefeš* to be serviced (Hadad). The psalm assumes loyalty to its kingly figure throughout; and it cultivates it. But in the end, its request faces toward the god and not toward any human, kingly legacy. Nonetheless, like the inscriptions, the psalm's request is most explicit in its closing lines. Psalm 2 is equally clear about the consequence of noncompliance, should the kings fail to serve Yhwh with fear: perishing. It is not a curse per se, but the psalm shares in common with its ancient counterparts that it closes with a threat.

No one is safer from this threat of divine harm than the king himself. Psalm 2 brooks no thought of Yhwh aggressing against his anointed. Such an idea runs counter to everything the psalm promotes; it is unthinkable within the psalm's rhetoric. This kingly exemption holds true even though the final sentence of the psalm widens its significance well beyond enemy kings – into the lives of anyone and everyone within reach of its rhetoric.

Psalm 2 concludes with a blessing: "Blessed are all who take refuge in him [i.e., Yhwh]." Because this line follows immediately from the threat, it can be construed as a continuation of the speech by the anonymous third party, the implicit nation of Yhwh, and addressed still to the seditious enemy kings. Taken together, these lines entertain two possible futures, one negative and one positive, much as the Hadad inscription; in effect they say: "Submit to Yhwh lest you perish – take refuge in Yhwh and be blessed." However, the fact that the closing line utters its blessing on *all* who take refuge puts the same choice that the enemy kings face in front of *whoever* reads or recites the psalm. The blessing is available to anyone; the final line democratizes such bliss. It also retroactively makes the adjuration to the kings binding on any reader or reciter. Even though they – we – are not directly targeted, still the psalm exhorts us, as if by proxy, to serve Yhwh with fear lest we perish. Divine aggression thus hangs over anyone who refuses to assume that posture.

Even so: the king is not included. Within the psalm, he is the absolute benchmark of divine blessing, at the furthest pole away from divine aggression. Far from incurring damage from Yhwh, Psalm 2 makes him the agent empowered by Yhwh to damage others, including the nations and the ends of the earth, presumably the domains of the kings who initially conspired against the duo of Yhwh and anointed.

Does Psalm 2, or other psalms like it, monotheize? It might seem like an unusual question, since on most accounts, Hebrew Scripture at large is monotheistic (and monotheizing). But the first section of the present Element argued that the exercise of distinguishing monotheism and polytheism is internal to the Jewish and Christian traditions, and indeed internal to the Bible: not all biblical texts monotheize, and certainly not all in the same way. At first glance, Psalm 2 seems like a promising candidate for a monotheizing text. It differs from the inscriptions examined earlier in that it names one god only, Yhwh; no list of gods appears in it. By a primarily numerical reckoning, this is a monotheistic text. Yet Section 1 also claimed that monotheizing is best gauged not by *counting* divine beings in a text but by *assessing their relationships*. Texts that monotheize concentrate sovereignty into one character, the supreme god; texts that do not monotheize are poly-sovereign. One god does not stand over against others or hold them in being at his discretion; they are self-standing agents, capable of countervailing.

Judged by these criteria, Psalm 2 is ambiguous. On the one hand, it binds the human king closely with Yhwh. They are introduced together as a team, albeit a strongly asymmetrical team in which one entity belongs to the other: Yhwh – and his anointed one. It also establishes the strongest imaginable bond between the king and the god: one of *sonship* and even *begetting*. The latter is a verb of generation. Used with female subjects, it denotes bearing in the womb and delivering. Used with male subjects, it indicates siring. Regardless: it is a bodily and a parental connection. It would seem strongly to limit whatever sovereignty God might exercise over against the kingly son; it endows the begotten with all the independence of any child vis-à-vis their parent. As noted, Psalm 2 makes the king the executor of Yhwh's will: far from being the potential recipient of divine aggression, he is Yhwh's reply to the rebellion of kings. He is Yhwh's hammer to break nations. All this is not very monotheizing.

But by the same token, the king's semidivine status is not a given, not primordial. Rather, it is bequeathed by Yhwh. The psalm is careful to point out that the sonship and begetting happen by *decree*. There is no scene of divine procreation, no psalmic rehearsal of theogony; there is instead the same noun that characterizes legal activities throughout the deuteronomistic materials, the laws and decrees that Israel must obey [*ḥoq;* more often plural in Deuteronomy, *ḥuqqim*]. The king's inheritance of nations must come by "asking" from Yhwh (v. 8). In these ways, the psalm's rhetoric protects the unique powers and prerogatives of one god.

The king's exemption from aggression perhaps weights the psalm toward a view of divine sovereignty that we might describe as less than monotheizing. Even if the kingly figure owes his existence to Yhwh's begetting, that same birthright protects him, in the psalm's rhetoric, from any possibility of divine destruction. Even if Yhwh exhorts him to ask for his worldwide inheritance, the force of the psalm is toward the inevitability of this power. No off-ramp or conditionality surrounds the king's status. At least in this text, he is safe, enjoying unshakable privileges befitting the begotten and beloved son of the patron god.

Psalm 89

Yet the Hebrew Psalter also contains a quite different perspective on the king: a more *monotheizing* one. In a few biblical psalms, the king is not exempt from divine aggression, and this liability to harm marks a heightened vision of divine sovereignty over against other beings. Divine power and privilege in these psalm texts do *not* extend to a human sub-regent. Power and privilege are textually limited, concentrated back onto the singular divine character, Yhwh. Psalm 89 presents the sharpest instance of this monotheizing rhetoric, and as such, a decisive theological development relative to the royal inscriptions and royal psalms that form its background. This psalm corroborates the thesis of the book: that monotheizing amplifies aggression. The god of this text is a more dangerous entity than his other, textualized counterparts, within the Psalter and beyond it.

The short opening stanza of Psalm 89, verses 1–5, introduces both its mood and its governing themes. It is – at first anyway – celebratory, and its focus is on Yhwh's "faithful acts" or "solicitous deeds," which are its very first words: "Of Yhwh's solicitous deeds, forever I will sing!" These acts quickly receive some further definition: they pertain to the covenant that Yhwh made with David (v. 4). The next and much longer stanza, verses 6–38, puts the establishment of David's dynasty within a much larger context; verses describe God's *founding of the cosmos*, crushing the primeval sea monster Rahab, ordering the world, creating North and South. These events coincide with the more particular acts concerning David; both are, in the end, a single, solicitous deed, world-making and dynasty-making at once. Yhwh speaks grand promises:

Then you spoke in a vision to your devoted ones | and you said:
"I set help on a warrior | I stood a chosen one up from the people.
I found David my servant | with my holy oil I anointed him.
My hand will be established with him | yes, my arm will strengthen him . . .
I will crush his foes from before him | and those who hate him I will strike down . . .
I set his hand on the Sea | and his right hand on the Rivers.
He will call on me: 'You are my father | My god and the rock of my salvation.'
As for me, I will make him firstborn | Most High among the kings of the earth."

The cosmogonic aggression against primeval enemies comes into the dynastic present. As Richard Clifford writes, "The same hand that defeated chaos and led the people in v. 14 is now with the chosen one in v. 22. Yahweh's defeat of his cosmic enemies [like Rahab] is reflected in the servant's defeat of his earthly foes in verses 23–24."[65] Yhwh also deputizes the aggression: "Sea and River, the enemies now tamed (vv. 10–11), are put under the power of the Davidide (v. 26)."[66] This is reminiscent of Psalm 2: Yhwh does not shatter the nations all by himself but empowers his anointed one to do it. So also as in Psalm 2, Yhwh authorizes David to call on him as *father*; like Tel Ahmar 6, the king is configured as the god's *firstborn*. Yhwh founded the world with all possible permanence and perpetuity; similarly, he ensures David's dynasty with the fullest suite of vocabulary for eternality: "I will set his offspring forever | and his throne like the days of heaven ... His offspring will continue forever | and his throne like the sun before me" (vv. 30, 37). All this has the effect of situating David and his descendants at the furthest possible remove, rhetorically, from danger of divine destruction.

The consistent direction of divine aggression in the psalm's first half – outward, away from the king, toward the god's ancient enemies and the king's foes – makes the succeeding stanza all the more shocking. The rhetorical *exemption* of the kingly persona from divine aggression, so characteristic of royal texts, adds to the jarring effect of what follows. In place of celebration, verses 39–46 intervene with sustained *accusation*:

But you – you have cast off and rejected | you have grown furious with your anointed
You have voided the covenant of your servant | you profaned his diadem to the ground
You breached all his walls | you made his fortress ruins ...
You lifted up the right hand of his foes | you caused all his enemies to rejoice
You have turned back the edge of his sword | you did not make him stand in battle
You have ended his radiance | his throne you threw to the ground
You shortened the days of his youth | you clothed him with shame.

Here divine aggression targets, not the god's enemies or the king's enemies, but the kingly person himself. The thought that was unthinkable for other royal texts comes raggedly to speech. Far from being exempted from harm, these verses toll out a series of verbs denoting damage, rejection, annulment, with the king as their object. Where positive verbs of help and rejoicing appear, they apply to the king's foes. Shortness replaces the dynastic durability of previous lines; shame replaces honor and primacy. In fact this stanza of accusation so neatly reverses the grand promises in the earlier part of the psalm that the latter are revealed as a foil; they are rhetorical setup. Psalm 89 plays up divine promises only in order to make its accusation sting more intensely. "Where now are your solicitous deeds from of old?" it asks God in conclusion (v. 50).

---

[65] Clifford, "Psalm 89," 36.   [66] Clifford, "Psalm 89," 36.

So radical were these verses of accusation that occasionally they came under censure in subsequent interpretive history. The medieval Spanish scholar Ibn Ezra knew of a "great and pious sage" who refused to read Psalm 89; Ibn Ezra himself agrees that it is blasphemous.[67] No other text of Hebrew Scripture imagines God "voiding" the covenant; and the extent of divine harm committed against the king is simply unparalleled. Still, Psalm 89 does not say that the biblical god *kills* the king, or injures his individual body. Divine violence is directed, rather, against the insignia of kingship: diadem, radiance, throne – these are overthrown. Military aid, the typical provision of the patron god, is withdrawn. City walls and fortresses, the building projects that mark out kingly accomplishment, are breached and ruined.

Psalm 89 is not monotheistic in the sense of featuring only one divine being. In comparison with Psalm 2, it shows a more populous heavenly world. The heavens thank God in verse 6. They are personified. The parallel line features a "congregation of holy ones" – gods – and verse 7, "sons of god(s)." At the same time, however, Psalm 89 endows an enormity of power and privilege into its kingly character – *only to evacuate it*. The king is child, even firstborn, of the god; he is agent of the god's own destructive power. Yhwh is invoked as the highest among the gods, "dreaded and feared to all who surround him"; but Yhwh promises the king, in strikingly godlike language, "I will make him Most High [*Elyon*] to the kings of earth" (v. 28b). In spite of this lofty start, these powers and privileges are rhetorically undone.

This evacuation is *monotheizing*. It leaves the highest human actor cast down, emptied out, scaled down. It lowers the *Elyon*, Most High, human king. It divests this potential sub-sovereign of that prerogative; and it leaves one divine sovereign standing in the text. This is why the final verses of Psalm 89 pray to God, reverting, textually, to the only one capable of remembering and rectifying David's humiliation. This psalm treats one god alone as god. In the process of de-divinizing David, it accuses this patron god of betrayal, reneging, and abasement. It is true that this textual god does not become lionlike, swallowing the heads of a perpetrator along with the heads of his wife and child. But in the end, apart from any absolute comparison of divine aggressiveness, the textual practice of monotheizing made the god of Psalm 89 more aggressive.

Conclusion: Literary Contexts and Counterbalances

The present section argued that a certain recurrent human character or "part" in ancient royal texts enjoys unique privileges, even divine sonship. As the begotten and beloved of the god, he is exempted from the god's destructiveness.

---

[67] Angel, "The Eternal Davidic Covenant," 85.

For royal inscriptions, and not a few royal biblical psalms, this is the unthinkable possibility. All other humans, from potential vandals to the king's own children, are in potential danger of the patron god – but not the king. However, in a few royal texts within Hebrew Scripture, this privilege and protection is withdrawn: the kingly person is subjected to divine aggression.[68] This evacuation is, the section argued, a form of monotheizing. It leaves one textual character, the biblical god, as the sole possessor and purveyor of power and safety, indeed as the sole salient agent. Psalm 89 provided the parade example of this subtractive mode of monotheizing.

And yet, as with the Flood Story of the previous section, this individual psalm text sits within a specific literary context. It does not offer its theological testimony in a vacuum, but rather, the editors of the Psalter have given it a particular role. Recent psalms research has brought attention to the placement of royal psalms at the "seams" of the five "books" within the Psalms anthology. Thus for example, Psalm 2, the royal psalm examined earlier, begins Book I of the Psalms; whatever its function was as an individual or independent composition (if it ever had one), it now acts as a "preface" to the whole Psalter, in concert with Psalm 1. It introduces the persona of the king as Yhwh's anointed, and it urges fealty to him. These serve, arguably, as coordinates for psalm materials that follow. Or again: Psalm 72 is a royal psalm set at the conclusion of Book II. Regardless its prior function, in the canonical presentation of the Psalter, it bookends, or transitions.

Similarly with Psalm 89: it is the last psalm within Book III of the Psalter. It closes a collection of psalms that are distinctively bleak within the whole psalm collection. Book III starts with the psalm of Asaph, Psalm 73, which recollects a near-miss ("my feet had almost stumbled, my steps had nearly slipped," 73:2) and recenters on the sanctuaries or holy places of God (Hebrew *miqdeš̂e*, 73:17). This same word for *sanctuary* reappears as a throughline in the brutal next psalm, Psalm 74, which recounts the destruction of the holy place, the hacking of its woodwork, its desecration and burning to the ground. It points to divine anger as the cause of these disasters, and it inquires plaintively after its reason (74:1). Rhetorical questions pepper this psalm, as well as the psalms following in Book III: just as the Asaph psalm raises questions to God ("How can God know?" 73:11a), Psalm 74 asks, "How long, O God, is the foe to scoff? Why do you hold back your hand?" (74:10a, 11a; cf. 79:5; 80:4[5]). The same kind of questioning and accusing and wondering surfaces in Psalm 89. Instead of destroyed *sanctuaries*, however, it looks back to the destruction of kingly

---

[68] For another example of a psalm that features divine aggression against the kingly person, see Psalm 132, on which Cornell, *Divine Aggression*, 169–178.

paraphernalia, city walls, public buildings. It is a fitting finale to this psalmic book of devastation. Together with Psalm 88, it constitutes the most somber and insistent psalm entry.

It also articulates the crisis to which the rest of the Psalter responds. In the judgment of many psalms scholars, Psalms 88 and 89 represent the lowest point, the apogee, of the whole corpus; the Books that follow then render up a slow-building, circuitous confession of trust in the face of disaster.[69] The entire Psalter thus works like an individual lament psalm, moving from complaint and petition to trust and praise. If this is so, then the monotheizing rhetoric of Psalm 89 is contextualized into the midpoint of the Psalter: it is made into an expression of the utmost theological crisis – and it is folded into a larger, rehabilitative arc. That is: psalms after it respond to it, reclaiming divine kingship, reorienting toward God's *torah* instruction, celebrating God's generosity to all of creation. These theo-logical moves do not de-monotheize. But they round out the only divine character that Psalm 89 leaves standing. They yield up a richer god-profile, and thereby make that sole deity, responsible for casting down even his beloved, kingly son, more sustainable and attractive. They provide context and counterbalance.

At the same time as the Psalter itself contextualizes the divine aggression against the king in Psalm 89, Jewish and Christian readers also layered theological expectations onto the figure of David's descendant. In some sense, their abundant and diverse ideas about *messiah* or *messiahs* reasserted the divine privilege and protection of the beloved royal son. If Psalm 89 evacuates these prerogatives, many texts of Second Temple Judaism reverse that flow: they once again exempt the Davidic heir from divine harm. They de-monotheize – not in a numerical sense but in their (re)distribution of divine sovereignty, textually considered.[70]

The relevant literature is far too vast to engage here.[71] But suffice it to say, the New Testament, understood as one such Second Temple cache, reactivates and repurposes the character of the kingly, Beloved Son: for example, at Jesus's baptism, the heavenly voice declares, "this is my Son, the Beloved" (Matt 3:17// Mark 1:11, Luke 3:22). The letters and gospels show that son succumbing to harm, perhaps even divine aggression, via crucifixion. But they also celebrate

---

[69] This insight traces back to Wilson, *Editing of the Hebrew Psalter*, 209–212; see also Wilson, "King, Messiah, and the Reign of God." The so-called "Shape and Shaping" school of psalm interpretation takes departure from and enriches this insight; see deClaissé-Walford, ed., *The Shape and Shaping of the Book of Psalms*, as well as now Prinsloo, "Reading the Masoretic Psalter as a Book."

[70] This is not to enter into pro- or anti-Trinitarian or divinity-of-Christ debates! Rather, the present argument points out that the New Testament, among other Jewish literature of the Second Temple period, pursues a very different repertoire of *literary* strategies vis-à-vis the Hebrew Bible. Like the Book of Watchers in 1 Enoch, it *textually* reconfigures the divine realm. See the previous section.

[71] But see Novenson, *The Grammar of Messianism*, also Henze, *Mind the Gap*, 53–85.

the heavenly session of the son, using language drawn from royal psalms (especially Psalm 110)[72]; and they emphasize the *invulnerability* of his transformed state: "since the *christos* was raised from the dead, he cannot die again; death no longer has dominion over Him" (Rom 6:9). In a word, the Beloved Son regains the kind of powerful and protected status that ancient counterparts like Hamiyatas or Pannamuwa once (textually) enjoyed.

4 Jealous God: National Annihilation

This final, fourth section of the Element considers another presentation of the biblical god's aggression. It is not, as in Section 2, the most extreme of all instances of divine aggression, the annihilation of all living beings through a worldwide flood. Nor is it, as in Section 3, the case of divine aggression catching up the character whom Yhwh would otherwise wholly support, namely, his human client king. Rather, the divine aggression examined here concerns *the people Israel*; and the destruction is not past but prospective (and prevented). God threatened to annihilate the chosen people after the debacle of the Golden Calf. The present section engages this threat of divinely wrought genocide.[73] The scale of the threat already suggests the unique intensity of the biblical god's aggressiveness. But the argument of this section is that the Golden Calf story reaches such a high water mark of aggression specifically through the rhetorical strategy of *monotheizing*. In other words, the biblical text makes Yhwh so destructive *in that* it concentrates all divine power and favor into this single divine character.

As with the previous section about the human king, the monotheizing of the Golden Calf story assumes an *evacuative* form. It does not *add* the powers of another god (or other gods) onto Yhwh's profile. This was the combinatory strategy of the biblical Flood Story in relation to its literary and theological precursors. Rather, the Golden Calf story *empties* other characters of the privilege and protection that they enjoy in other textual circumstances. Perhaps contrary to a more conventional or surface-level reading of the Golden Calf story, the literary evacuation of divine status that the present section investigates does not pertain to the statue itself. In a section on monotheism and monotheizing, this calf statue might seem like the more obvious candidate for treatment under these coordinates: Aaron fashions it as a rival god, or a representation of a rival god, or a rival representation of the biblical god, and then the biblical text demonstrates the calf's powerlessness relative to Yhwh. Moses burns it with

---

[72] Hay, *Glory at the Right Hand.*
[73] See Kugler, *When God Wanted.* In using the (fraught and, in the context of the Bible, contested) word genocide, I follow Kugler's example. See also Kugler, "Metaphysical Hatred."

fire, grinds it to powder, mixes it in water, and forces the Israelites to drink it up (Exod 32:20). This would appear to amount to a textually effected evacuation of a rival claimant to divine power! One that leaves Yhwh as the sole textual proprietor of divinity.

But the present section considers another and subtler emptying: not of the calf but of *the people of Yhwh*, the nation of Israel. In the Golden Calf story, *the entire community* is positioned as covenant partner of the deity, and as such, it is able *collectively* to incur the punishments following from violation of covenant stipulations. The people, taken as a whole, fill the expected role of divine protection and patronage that the text ferociously evacuates.

After laying out the Golden Calf story, especially its covenantal framing, the section looks at a couple of other biblical texts where divine aggression does not foreground this framing to such an extent, and where divine destructiveness therefore does not reach so exhaustive a scale; possibly, too, these other biblical texts lie in the developmental background of the Exodus 32 calf story, though that is not the section's main burden to exposit. The present section also considers another body of ancient texts, the Neo-Assyrian Vassal Treaties, to indicate how their concept of *covenantal* terms and penalties compares to the Golden Calf story. The section furthermore describes the theological effects of Exodus making the client nation, not an automatically safe and protected entity, but a covenant signatory liable to divine harm. As in previous sections, it closes by considering the literary contexts and counterbalances of this biblical instance of divine aggression.

The Golden Calf Story

The Golden Calf story appears in Exodus 32. This section tells the story of scripture's very deepest debacle: the arch-sin of Israel, their reneging of the covenant at the moment of its forging.[74] According to the canonical presentation of the Book of Exodus, this catastrophe takes place at Mount Sinai. Moses's whole career has faced toward this site: back in Exodus 3, Yhwh called to him from the midst of the burning bush – a word whose Hebrew form suggests the place-name to which he will later return: *saneh*, bush, anticipating *Sinai*, the mountain, and the fire iconically anticipating the fiery presence of God that will blaze again in the sight of all the people.[75] From the fire, Yhwh promises to deliver Israel out of hard service to Egypt; and Yhwh commissions Moses to

---

[74] Helpful readings of the story from which the present section drew insight are Childs, *Exodus*, 553–581; Aberbach and Smolar, "Aaron, Jereboam, and the Golden Calves"; and Hayes, "Golden Calf Stories."

[75] I owe this point about the iconicity of the fire to Moberly, *God of the Old Testament*, 55–56.

bring them back to this very mountain to service Yhwh there. Intervening chapters narrate these decisive stories.

In chapter 19, the people arrive at the foot of the mountain. Moses ascends (19:3a) and receives a message from Yhwh, the first of many given to him from the mountaintop. This initial Sinai speech of Yhwh to Moses features the Hebrew word for covenant (*berit*); it is the first occurrence of the word in the Book of Exodus in connection with a different, newer covenant than the one God made long beforehand with the ancestors Abraham, Isaac, and Jacob (see Exod 2:24; 6:4, 5). This new covenant in Exodus comes with a condition. It takes the form, in English, of an *if*, addressed to the people, and a *then* following, specifying a beneficent divine action: "*if* you obey my voice and keep my covenant, *then* you shall be my treasured possession out of all the peoples" (19:5). The elders of the people agree to these terms: "all that Yhwh has spoken, we will do!" (19:8).

All this is in preparation for Yhwh's descent upon the top of the mountain, a mysterious, visually and aurally overwhelming event that the end of Exodus chapter 19 describes. Yhwh comes down and bequeaths Moses the Ten Commandments. In first position, these foundational words stipulate that Israel shall have no other gods beside Yhwh; and they shall not make a sculptured image (20:2, 3; cf. 20:20). Numerous further legal directions follow. Moses recites these materials back to Israel; significantly, they are identified as covenantal: "[Moses] took the *book of the covenant* and read it in the hearing of the people" (24:7). Twice in response to Moses's reading the people commit to their obligations: "All the words that Yhwh has spoken, we will do!" (24:3, 7). Moses solemnizes the pact by spattering the blood of slaughtered animals on the people; Exodus calls it the *blood of the covenant* (24:8).

It is during Moses's next ascent up the mountain that the Golden Calf story occurs. He made the trek at Yhwh's behest, to receive from God *stone tablets* containing yet more instruction and commandments for the people (24:12; 31:18). He lingered there forty days and nights. Chapter 32 begins with the scene that happens in his absence at the bottom of the mountain. The people make a request of Aaron: "Come, make gods for us, who shall go before us; as for this Moses, the man who brought us up out of the land of Egypt, we do not know what has become of him" (32:2). Aaron obliges. He orders the people to donate their gold, and, having received it, he fashions it with an engraving tool into the shape of a calf. Aaron declares to them: "This is your God [*elohim*], O Israel, who brought you up from the Land of Egypt" (32:4b). He institutes a festival to Yhwh (32:5).

This biblical chapter is relevant to the theme of divine aggression (and mono-theizing) because of the content that then follows. The narrative pans back to the top of the mountain. Yhwh makes two alarmed speeches to Moses. In the first and shorter speech, Yhwh informs Moses that the people have *corrupted* themselves – the same verb used of all people on earth in the Flood Story (Gen 6:11–13). In verbiage that closely echoes the narrator's own telling, Yhwh reports to Moses the making of the molten calf as well as Aaron's announcement, "this is your God." Yhwh urges Moses to *hurry down* the mountain.

In his second and longer speech (vv. 7–14), Yhwh makes a different exhortation to Moses: not to *hurry down* – but to *leave me alone*. The command emerges from a dark vision that Yhwh has had; and he shares it with Moses: "I see this people – and look, it is a hard-necked people" (32:8). It is not an observation of what the people have *done*, corrupting themselves by their activity; it is an observation about what this people is *like*: hard-necked, obstinate, impervious to instruction. Because of this divine insight into Israel's incorrigibility, Yhwh says (32:9):

> So now, *leave me alone*, that my anger may flare against them and I may destroy them; but I will make of you a great nation.

Yhwh's opening speech to Moses on the mountaintop concerned his clientage and proprietorship of the entire people: "you shall be my treasured possession." But this status depended on the people's fulfillment of the major condition, the *if* statement to which the elders agreed: "*if* you obey my voice and keep my covenant." In the literary presentation of the Book of Exodus, the people have through the Golden Calf incident reneged exactly on this term: they have not heeded the divine voice or kept covenant with Yhwh, and so Yhwh correspondingly says he will cancel out their status. They will not be his treasured possession. More than that: he will consume them.

Moses intercedes for the people, appealing to Yhwh's reputation among the Egyptians as well as to Yhwh's past promises to Israel. He prays for Yhwh to turn from his fierce anger and to *repent* from this evil that he threatens on his people. Verse 11 of the chapter frames Moses's activity piquantly; in Everett Fox's translation, "Moses soothed the face of Yhwh his God." And Moses's pleas prevail, such that Yhwh does repent of the evil he said he would do to his people (32:14).[76]

In spite of this turnabout, all is not well thereafter. Moses himself experiences a surge of anger; he smashes the tablets that God's own finger had inscribed. He burns the calf and forces the people to drink it. He responds to the chaos with an all-too-lethal form of crowd control. Yhwh sends a plague. Even so, in the following chapter, Yhwh's temper is barely contained. He repeats his dark observation about the obduracy of the people: "I myself will not go up in your midst, for you are a hard-necked people, lest I destroy you on the way"

---

[76] Fox, *The Five Books of Moses*, 444; also Sonnet, "God's Repentance."

(33:3; cf. again in 33:5). The threat of divine annihilation lingers. Eventually Yhwh accepts this people as his own, mercifully exceeding the initial terms of his initial if-then proposal. In spite of the people's breach of obedience, Yhwh continues on with them.

But for purpose of assessing divine aggression in the Golden Calf story, it is important to register the radicality of Yhwh's destructive threat. The god's response is immediate; his destructive intent, all-inclusive. And the *covenantal framing* of the story is indispensable for understanding these dimensions of Yhwh's wrath. In Exodus's canonical presentation, Yhwh's ferocity is intelligible because of the people's consent to the terms of their pact. Without such if-then scaffolding, Yhwh's rage would be opaque, irrational, excessive. In the canonical text, *covenant* provides the rationale. It heightens the people's responsibility; it brings their *deserving* into focus. It also amplifies sovereignty, by loading discretion onto God: the people's life or death is placed into his hands.

The example of other biblical texts is clarifying in this regard: they show similar, even very similar sins as the Golden Calf story, but Yhwh's aggression does not in them reach so radical a scale. Significantly, the literarily smaller-sized wrath they depict corresponds to their literarily more modest reliance on covenant as a theme and organizing concept. The first comparable story also features calf statues – not one of them but two. 1 Kings 12 tells of King Jeroboam.[77] It is but one episode within a long and tragic arc cascading out from David's sin with Bathsheba, descending through Solomon's apostasy, and into the folly of his heir, Rehoboam. In response to Rehoboam's hubris and excess, the northern tribes break away, and Jeroboam is their upstart king. He realizes, however, that his people's religious life still centers on the worship of Yhwh in Jerusalem, which could undercut his new national project. He therefore enacts a religious recentering: not toward a different god per se – but toward different worship objects and different, northerly worship sites. He creates two golden calves, and, as the Hebrew text has it, he announces them to the people in words virtually identical to Aaron's: "Here are your gods [*elohim*], Israel, who brought you up out of Egypt!" (1 Kgs 12:28). Like Aaron, Jeroboam also inaugurates a festival, or rather, festivals. He installs priests who are not Levites.

In parallel fashion to the Golden Calf story of Exodus, there is an immediate divine response to Jereboam's act: while Jeroboam himself is making an offering at his newly founded calf shrines, a "man of God" receives a word from Yhwh. Yhwh promises through this word that Jeroboam's illicit altar will later split; and a later king named Josiah will desecrate it. The end of the same chapter

---

[77] See again Aberbach and Smolar, "Aaron, Jereboam, and the Golden Calves."

declares that Jeroboam's appointment of illegitimate priests is the sin of "the house of Jeroboam that led to its downfall and to its destruction from the face of the earth" (13:34). The following chapter contains another divine message. Yhwh promises again to destroy Jeroboam's dynasty, here specifically because of his creation of the molten calves: "You have done more evil than all who lived before you. You have made for yourself other gods, idols made of metal; you have aroused my anger and turned your back on me. Because of this, I am going to bring disaster on the house of Jeroboam" (14:9–10a).

In the long and tragic arc of 1–2 Kings, Jeroboam becomes the archetypical evil king, the reference point for all subsequent kings in their failure to comply with Yhwh's commandments. Of note, however, is the relatively more targeted scope of Yhwh's destructiveness in these messages to Jeroboam: through prophetic messengers, the biblical god threatens Jeroboam's *altar*(s); he pledges to destroy Jeroboam's *house* and to turn the kingship over to someone else. Even these events do not happen right away; the altar is not desecrated for generations, and Jeroboam reigns many years after fashioning the calves. True, his sin is paradigmatic for subsequent unrighteous kings, and in a certain sense, his establishment of the northern calf cult generates the eventual capsizing of the whole nation. But the book traces the roots of that disaster back much further than him, to the reigns of Israel's greatest kings, and it spreads responsibility across numerous subsequent kingly agents, in successive, compounding generations.

Possibly the Golden Calf story depends literarily on Jeroboam's calves. Scholarly opinion is united in the opinion that these two texts are genetically related; it is somewhat divided when it comes to the direction of descent (i.e., which story came first).[78] Regardless the answer to that question of composition history, the Golden Calf story lays responsibility far more on the *whole people.* They initiate; Aaron caves to them. And the Golden Calf story visits the ensuing threat of divine destruction far more directly on the people: the object of Yhwh's wrath is the nation as a whole.

In Kings, by contrast, Jeroboam's *dynasty* is the immediate object of Yhwh's wrath, the nation in a much more complex and extended sense. Covenantal framing is present in the Jeroboam text; after all, the good king Josiah who desecrates the altar does so precisely in compliance with *the book of the covenant* (2 Kgs 22–23). But in comparison with the Golden Calf story, the Jeroboam story does not foreground covenant obligations. The if-then is not stated proximately and forthrightly, and insofar as there are signatories to an agreement with God, they are not the entire people in assembly. The text's

---

[78] See Hayes, "Golden Calf Stories."

vision of responsibility is, rather, multiplex: a series of kings, a chain of events, a pileup of generations. Its comparative backgrounding of covenant, and its more distributed agency, match the long delay and multiple targets of Yhwh's destructiveness in Kings.

Conversely, the immediacy and comprehensiveness of Yhwh's threatened aggression in the Golden Calf story dovetail with its covenantal framing. Cross-referencing the story with Jeroboam's calves showcases this theological relationship, because in Kings, the god's aggression is longer-term and more targeted – and covenant plays a more modest role. Much the same can be said of the story of Gideon's ephod in Judges chapter 8, except that in it, covenant is even less of a governing concept, and divine aggression is even more dilute and delayed.[79] The Gideon story begins with controversy over leadership. In this it is alike to both the Golden Calf story and the story of Jeroboam's calves: the people approach Aaron in Moses's absence; Jeroboam is concerned to reroute the people's devotion away from Jerusalem and David's dynasty that rules from Jerusalem. In Judges 8:22, the Israelites say to Gideon, "Rule over us, you and your son and your grandson also, for you have delivered us out of the hand of Midian!" Gideon refuses, insisting on Yhwh's sole rule over the people.

But Gideon does then make a request: "Each of you give me an earring he has taken as spoil" (8:24b). The narrator then inserts an explanatory parenthesis: "For the enemy had golden earrings because they were Ishmaelites" (8:24c). The verb by which Gideon commands the people ("give") is distinct from Aaron's command ("take off"), but the words for golden earrings are nearly identical (Hebrew: *nizmê-zahav*). The metal out of which Aaron fashions the calf and out of which Gideon fashions the ephod are the same; possibly they are both *booty*, which is to say, treasure taken by force from non-Israelite peoples, Egyptians and Midianites, respectively.[80] In both stories, the people oblige their leader's command: the Israelites give over their gold to Gideon, just as they gave it over to Aaron at Mount Sinai. Gideon then makes an ephod, a kind of sacred garment, or perhaps a portable cult object, and he *sets up* this object in his home city of Ophrah. The same Hebrew verb for *setting up* describes what the Philistines do to the captured ark inside of their temple: they place it nearby the statue of their god Dagon so that he can look upon it (1 Sam 5:2). Or again: the same verb describes what the Israelites do when they place the ark inside the tabernacle (2 Sam 6:17). It is a verb of sacred installation.

Laconically, the narrative then reports the results of Gideon's ephod installation: "all Israel prostituted themselves to [the ephod] there, and it became

---

[79] The treatment by Aaron, *Etched in Stone*, 234–244, brought the Gideon story to my attention.
[80] Aaron, *Etched in Stone*, 234–244.

a snare to Gideon and to his family" (Judg 8:27b). This verse communicates the narrator's harshly negative judgment on Gideon's work. The word *prostituted* evokes sexual transgression or infidelity. Such a gendered concept of wayward-ness only obtains when some benchmark of right conduct, a standard of integrity or fidelity, is up and running. It seems historically that Israel's prophetic literature first mobilized this *marital metaphor*; the narrator of the Gideon story only touches upon it, activates it – but does not explicate or explain it. It remains implicit, in the background, a rhetorical nod. *Covenant* as a concept lives in close proximity to this marital metaphor: both comprise a pact demanding mutual loyalty, and both presume penalties for reneging. But in no way is covenant the basic, overt, structuring idea of this Judges passage as it is in the Golden Calf story. At most, covenant is but a hint in the Gideon story. The other word in the Gideon text by which the narrator spells out the consequence of Gideon's ephod is *snare*. This term suggests a long-term problem. A snare is a trap: it lies ready to spring on its target. It is harmful, but it is not activated immediately.

Divine aggression in the Gideon story does not arrive quickly on the heels of the sin it narrates. Nor is its recipient immediately obvious: the whole people go astray after the ephod, it is a snare – but Gideon, the creator of the cult object, dies at a good old age (Judg 8:32). The people themselves do not perish straightaway, neither do they experience subjugation, at least for some time after this event. In comparison to the other two stories, the Golden Calf and Jeroboam's calves, the biblical god's response to Gideon's ephod is even more muted. There is no immediate command to God's representative to *hurry down*, no request to *leave me alone*. There is no immediate message of doom for Gideon's household, communicated through a man of God. Whatever wrath befalls because of the golden ephod, it is delayed, and its targets, dilute. Aggression moves subterraneanly through the narrative rather than erupting volcanically at its surface as in the Golden Calf story. All this demonstrates the interlocking and proportionality of covenantal framing and divine aggression.

Neo-Assyrian Vassal Treaties and Monotheizing

The Golden Calf story remembers a radical example of divine aggression, when Yhwh's wrath threatened to annihilate the entire people of Israel.[81] The imme-diacy and the scope of his destructiveness stand out relative to more postponed and more specifically earmarked examples of divine aggression in otherwise similar biblical texts. The section has argued that the intensity of textualized divine aggression is proportional to those texts' dependence on covenant as

---

[81] See again Kugler, *When God Wanted*.

a literary framing. Putting a solemn, binding contract between the god and the people at the literary forefront helps to make sense of the god's upset, and allows for more of it: the people have reneged on the terms to which they agreed. This provides a rationale and a license for the god's destructiveness. However, if it is clear that "covenantalizing" corresponds to a more textually amplified divine aggression, it is not yet clear how covenantalizing relates to *monotheizing*. Granted that divine wrath is faster and more ferocious in the Golden Calf episode, does this story *monotheize*, especially in comparison to these similar but somewhat less divinely aggressive biblical stories?

The present section offers an affirmative answer. But the connection between covenant and monotheizing can be seen more clearly by drawing in another body of texts, this time from outside the Bible: the Neo-Assyrian Vassal Treaties. These documents are also known by the emic term *adê*, the Akkadian word used to refer to "sworn pacts of loyalty imposed by the Assyrian emperor on his vassals."[82] In these texts, a human superpower, the Assyrian emperor, articulates terms of an agreement between himself and an inferior king or nation. The emperor foists many responsibilities onto the lesser party. Their language of *listening* to the sovereign's voice and *keeping* the sovereign's *commands* mirrors that of Deuteronomy – as well as Yhwh's first speech to Moses on the mountain:

Exod 19:5:	If you *listen* to my voice and *keep* my covenant
Deut 13:18:	If you *listen* to the voice of Yhwh your God by *keeping* all his commandments that I am commanding you today
VTE 195:	You shall *listen* to whatever [the king] says and *do* whatever he commands, and you shall not seek any other king or any other lord against him.[83]

Exclusive loyalty is the foremost concern of the Vassal Treaty to demand of the vassal. These *adê* texts adjure their signatories to protect the imperial heir (§5); to report on any sedition or treason (§§6, 10); to join in putting down revolt (§14) and escaping from rebels (§15). Above all, the vassal shall have no other kings beside the Assyrian emperor: they are forbidden from swearing oaths to other lords, also from engaging with statues of other lords, since such activity would bind them to rivals. The Succession Treaty of Esarhaddon reads as follows:

> *VTE* 123: You shall not do (anything) that is evil and improper to Assurbanipal the great crown prince designate, whom Esarhaddon, king of Assyria, your lord, has ordered for you; you shall not seize him and put him to

---

[82] Parpola and Watanabe, *Neo-Assyrian Treaties*, xv.
[83] Parpola and Watanabe, *Neo-Assyrian Treaties*, 36.

death, nor hand him over to his enemy, nor oust him from the kingship of Assyria, nor swear an oath to any other king or any other lord.

VTE 123: You shall not take a mutually binding oath with (any)one who installs (statues of) gods in order to conclude a treaty before gods, (be it) by sett[ing] a table, by drinking from a cup, by kindling a fire, by water, by oil, or by holding breasts.

Compare the first command(s) of the Decalogue, also known as the Ten Words, given by Yhwh to Moses, which similarly prohibits other lords and manufacture of statuary:

Exod 20:3–5a: You shall have no other gods before me. You shall not make for yourself an idol, whether in the form of anything that is in heaven above or that is on the earth beneath or that is in the water under the earth. You shall not bow down to them or serve them, for I the Lord your God am a jealous God.[84]

Notably, the vassals consent to the *adê* stipulations; they make a public oath, with many gods as witnesses to it. The Vassal Treaty supplies them with words in the first-person plural ("we"): "we will not make rebellion or insurrection against Esarhaddon, king of Assyria . . . may all the gods mentioned by name hold us, our seed and our seed's seed accountable (for this vow)" (*VTE* §57). Furthermore, the list of responsibilities is put on repository. The pact is inscribed onto official *tablets* (Akkadian *ṭuppi-adê*, tablets of the treaty or oath). The vassal is commanded: "You shall guard this treaty tablet which is sealed with the seal of Aššur, king of the gods, and set up in your presence, like your own god" (*VTE* §35). The *adê* pact was, finally, solemnized through sacrifice. In effect if not terminologically, animal blood ratified the agreement. Finally, the Vassal Treaties conclude with a fearsome roster of curses: a veritable catalogue of divine aggression is listed out, should the vassals renege. An if-then premise drives the whole treaty form. Failing to uphold stipulations results in divinely prosecuted doom for the vassal.

Biblical scholars have for generations noticed the resemblances between ancient Near Eastern treaties and the Sinai covenant.[85] The repertoire of elements – a demand for exclusive loyalty from a sovereign of an inferior, a public oath ceremony, tablets and blood, the threat of annihilation conditional on noncompliance – is too similar for coincidence. Even the word used for Israel as Yhwh's "treasured possession" finds a counterpart in Akkadian *adê* literature.[86] The conviction that biblical texts about *covenant* and *covenant-making* reflect an

---

[84] Otto, *Das Deuteronomium*; also Weinfeld, "Traces of Assyrian Treaty Formulae"; Frankena, "The Vassal-Treaties of Esarhaddon."

[85] See Mendenhall, "Covenant Forms in Israelite Tradition"; Thompson, *The Ancient Near Eastern Treaties and the Old Testament.*

[86] Greenberg, "Hebrew *segulla*: Akkadian *sikiltu*."

ancient, shared notion, rather than an innovation distinctive to ancient Judah and Israel, is therefore widely accepted. What scholars debate is when exactly covenant came to occupy a central place in ancient Israel's thinking; and the kinds of treaties that most influenced the Hebrew Bible's covenantal presentations of Yhwh vis-à-vis Israel.

The present section cannot hope to adjudicate such complex matters.[87] For sake of arguing that the Golden Calf story *monotheizes*, however, the historical relationship between the Sinai materials in Exodus and the Vassal Treaties need not be resolved. It may well be that Exodus is conceptually downstream from the Assyrian *adê* literature; this would be the case if, in turn, Deuteronomy adapts Assyrian treaty language and concepts, and the exchange between Yhwh and Moses in Exodus 32:7–14 is deuteronomistic (in Childs's words: "verses 7–14 are saturated with Deuteronomic language"[88]). But we do not need a genealogical flowchart between Exodus and the Assyrian *adê* in order to observe their *phenomenological* parallels. They *work* similarly. Their rhetorics seek a comparable goal: the exclusive loyalty of the lesser party to the imperial figure.

Section 1 of the present Element considered "roles" or "parts" that characters play in various texts. It proposed to attend not only or firstly to terminology that communicates divine anger but rather to a bundle of features that are transferable across texts. Section 2 thus noticed the role of the grieving, conflicted, and memorializing (mother)-god(dess): this persona in one text, the Atrahasis Epic, is traceable in the other, the Book of Genesis. In a similar way, the "part" of emperor functions similarly in both the Vassal Treaties and the Book of Exodus. In a real way, the writings about the Sinai covenant transpose Yhwh into the human sovereign. Israelites enter into a sworn pact with him; they agree to abide by the god's commandments and they accept the if-then premise, such that reneging will void their status as treasured possession. When the Golden Calf debacle occurs, it is morally legible exactly because of this context – this covenantal framework.

Putting Yhwh into the literary role of emperor (and making Israel his "vassal") has several theological effects. But *monotheizing* is an apt shorthand for them. One theological effect of casting Yhwh as emperor, perhaps the most powerful effect, is to emphasize his sole lordship: he alone is the king to whom Israel owes allegiance. Any others are forbidden. Even simulacra of others, statues and images, and the rites and festivals pertaining to them, are off limits, just as statues of other kings are off limits to the vassals of Esarhaddon ("You shall not take a mutually binding oath with (any)one who installs (statues of) gods"). The other theological effect of textualizing Yhwh as emperor is to increase Yhwh's

---

[87] See still, Nicholson, *God and His People.*
[88] Childs, *Exodus*, 559; similarly Kugler, *When God Wanted*, 25.

discretion over Israel's life and death. Their thriving, even their existence, are given over to his choice. The people live at Yhwh's good pleasure, and they perish at his will. Deuteronomy reproduces many of the curse formulations that the Vassal Treaties line out. Exodus narrates the prospect of divine destruction ensuing from covenant noncompliance. This kind of power to harm fits the present Element's (Section 1) definition of monotheizing: "That god, the supreme god, may conscript them at his discretion, or destroy them at will. The one god holds the others in existence or wills them into nonexistence." This description pertains quite clearly to the god of the Golden Calf story, and the imperial personification makes a key contribution to that profile. "Imperializing" Yhwh leaves a single, sole textual sovereign.

The manner in which the Golden Calf story monotheizes is not numerical. Other gods appear besides Yhwh, just as other, rival human sovereigns appear in the Vassal Treaties. Both documents are pervasively concerned to forestall any errant devotion to these competitors. They are off limits: real but *verboten*. But these texts also legitimate the sovereign's power over the existence of his underlings. Should harm befall them, even divine destruction, it is licit, expected, sensible: after all, the vassal characters consented, uttering together, we will! They are thus conscripted, textually, as cosigners of the divine aggression that catches them up. They are agents, and remain agents in the presentation of the text. But they are agents that have signed over their right to life to another character. They are, as it were, *emptied* of whatever safety and protection to which they might otherwise be entitled: they are left without self-determination and vulnerable to the sovereign's punishing hand. Such is the monotheizing of the Golden Calf; and it finds no counterpart in the other biblical texts examined in the chapter, because they rely less intensively on a covenantal framing.

Conclusions: Literary Contexts and Counterbalances

The present chapter examined the Golden Calf story: a narrative in which the biblical god threatens to consume the whole people of Israel that he had brought out of Egypt. This threat yields up a premier instance of divine aggression. The chapter next demonstrated through comparison that *covenant* undergirds the radicality of Yhwh's aggression in the Golden Calf stories: other biblical texts such as Jeroboam's calves or Gideon's ephod show characters sinning by fashioning golden statuary, yet they do not show a comparable immediacy or comprehensiveness of divine destructiveness. The chapter pointed to the relatively more modest role of covenant in these scriptural passages as a feature complementary to their more modest rendition of Yhwh's aggression. Finally, the chapter looked at Neo-Assyrian Vassal Treaties as an ancient comparand and proposed that the literary character of Yhwh functions similarly to the

Assyrian emperor: as a sovereign – to whom the people are exclusively bound by oath; and who exercises legitimate power over the people's life and death. The threat of divinely wrought doom hangs over both the Exodus and the *adê* texts: it is the penalty for reneging. Whatever safety and benevolence a community might enjoy in other textual configurations of nation vis-à-vis deity, in such covenantal literature, it is removed. This evacuation is, as with the evacuation of kingly privilege in the Section 3, a "mode" of monotheizing.

The Golden Calf story is, in its literary context, a singular event. Sinai is the epicenter of the Torah: the heart of the whole Pentateuch, when God gives the Law over to Moses and through him to the people of Israel; and when God's own *kabôd* presence descends into the tabernacle. These chapters lay out the foundational moments of Israel's life. Their relevance is eternal, but not because they enunciate a divine manifestation that Israel and claimants to Israel's heritage expect to happen again. God will not "act like this" again. The disclosure of the Law is once and for all; and this disaster at the foot of the mountain, because it is ensconced there, is unique and unrepeatable. There will never again be a time when Moses is absent from Israel and they have not yet received the Law. In this way, Yhwh's threat to wipe out the people belongs, like the Flood Story of Genesis, to the primeval past. It is not a live threat, because its originary moment has passed.

It is also, literarily, a divine threat that Moses's intercession overcomes. That is to say: Yhwh's initiative to annihilate the chosen people and start over is always and already prevented. Moses succeeded in soothing the divine face. Yhwh repented. As Jean-Pierre Sonnet argues, Yhwh repents at three crucial places in Hebrew Scripture: at the flood, at the Golden Calf, and at Saul's kingship.[89] But Yhwh doesn't just turn away from the dire possibility he had raised to Moses. In the presentation of the Book of Exodus, the Golden Calf story ends with an unprecedented revelation of Yhwh's character. In chapter 34, the tablets are remade. Yhwh restarts the covenant. And he gives Moses a profound new description of who he is:

> Yhwh! Yhwh!
> A God compassionate and gracious
> A God abounding in faithfulness and truth
> Keeper of faithfulness to thousands
> Forgiver of iniquity, transgression, and sin!
> One who does not leave wrongdoing unpunished!
> Repayer of parental guilt
> > to children, even grandchildren
> > to the third, even the fourth generation![90]

---

[89] Sonnet, "God's Repentance."   [90] Translation follows Strawn, "Yhwh's Poesie," 38.

In this charter statement, Yhwh is unbalanced. His graciousness cascades down on a thousand generations, whereas he visits destruction only to the fourth generation. Insofar as the threat against the people in Exodus maps onto this declaration, it must be counterweighted by a proportionately far greater divine faithfulness. Or so the literary context would suggest! This is a significant containment and curtailment of the divine aggressiveness that the text entertains. It is also a complication to the imperial image of Yhwh that the Sinai materials otherwise repurpose. The composite Yhwh of the canonical text bears many affinities with the Assyrian emperor. But there is no comparative equivalent to Moses's intercession and to Yhwh's pronunciation of his name. In these regards, the biblical text goes beyond its antique precursor (or: lookalike), building a different kind of reciprocity and compassion into the sovereign's profile.

This enrichment of Yhwh's persona does not de-monotheize. His recital of his name to Moses does not undo the sovereignty that the previous materials line out. Instead it leaves a suppler and more gracious single, textual sovereign. Still life and death are in the hands of this one; the people do not forget that Yhwh can revoke their status as treasured possession, and indeed, several other biblical texts reprise much the same scene of divine threat.[91] Even if the moment at the foot of Sinai is unrepeatable, and Yhwh's character is weighted toward mercy, genocide is a peril that hovers across many biblical texts. And, because of covenantal frameworks that structure much of Hebrew Scripture, this peril was understood, in some places at least, as the result of the people's reneging. The rhetorics of these texts access this fear of deconstitution and destruction – in order to incentivize the practice of faithfulness toward Yhwh. As Section 1 noted, there is a strongly existential dimension to the Hebrew Bible's depictions of divine aggression, and hence, too, of its monotheizing.[92]

Other and subsequent receptions of the Golden Calf and its threat of annihilation at God's hands do effect a kind of de-monotheizing. As previous sections have observed, Jewish and Christian readers did not reiterate the literary strategies of concentrating divinity that the Hebrew Bible exemplifies. If the Book of Exodus evacuates the people of Israel of safety and self-determination they would otherwise possess, other early Jewish and Christian writings replenish the people of God with these qualities. Some texts even freight the people of God, the inheritors of Israel's name and legacy, with qualities of divinity, assuming that safety from divine aggression comprises, as the present section argues, one such quality.

A striking example of this phenomenon is the use of "body of *christos*" imagery in the New Testament, considered as a specimen of Second Temple

---

[91] Kugler, *When God Wanted.*   [92] Moberly, "How Appropriate Is Monotheism?"

literature. Ernst Käsemann noticed long ago that the apostle Paul writes of Christ's body only in his ethical exhortations. By contrast, the (likely post-Pauline) letters to the Colossians and Ephesians move the body of Christ up into their opening theological sections, into praise and prayer itself, even into Christology proper. They spatialize the person of *christos*, extending him so that his self contains the addressees. They lend the people of God a certain measure of autonomy, as Käsemann says: "the theme of the church moves into the centre and takes on independent life."[93] Literarily, these letters *christify* the people of God. Perhaps and as such they even (re)*divinize* the people of God.

The use of "body of *christos*" conceptually counteracts whatever jeopardy of divine aggression earlier forms of covenantal framing entail. It is fitting for an emperor to threaten harm on vassals in the event that they serve other lords: this is the moral intelligibility of the Golden Calf episode. But it is not at all fitting for the head of a body to act harmfully against his own body. The Letter to the Ephesians lofts this exact possibility only to foreclose it and show its incoherence. It reads: "No one ever hates his own body, but he nourishes and tenderly cares for it, just as *christos* does for the church, because we are members of his body" (5:29–30).

The point is not that Colossians and Ephesians are receiving and responding to the Golden Calf story. I am aware of no echoes of that Hebrew Scripture text within these letters. Instead, as with prior sections, the larger contention is that Jewish and Christian writings move away from the monotheizing model that Hebrew Scripture deploys. In Exodus, the people of God are exposed to annihilating divine aggression in view of their subscription to the covenant. Monotheizing endangers them; their title to safety is literarily *evacuated*. In these letters, however, the people of God are not exposed to divine aggression. To the contrary, whatever divine privileges and prerogatives pertain to the *christos*, these texts are at pains to emphasize that *christos*-followers share in them. Their membership in his body affords them protection. In this sense, these epistles de-monotheize.[94]

5 Conclusions, Questions, and Future Directions

This Element makes an argument in three case studies: that monotheism aggrandizes divine aggression. Or, rather, that textual strategies of *monotheizing*, making

---

[93] Käsemann, "The Motif of the Body of Christ," 120.

[94] As with Section 3, the present argument does not enter into intra-Christian theological dispute about theosis or divinization. Its focus is literary and comparative: these writings from the New Testament corpus do not monotheize the people of God, reserving divine safety to Yhwh alone, in the same way as Exodus.

one character the sovereign and sole salient deity, has the follow-on effect of increasing that deity's aggression. The Element examined two "modes" by which this monotheizing and hence "aggressifying" occurs. First, an *aggregative* or combinatory mode. Texts that pursue this strategy absorb divine roles ("parts") that are elsewhere independent into the one god. This results in a more complex and composite god. It also means that formerly independent, destructive agents are folded into the singular god character; hence he becomes more aggressive. The first case study of the Flood Story showcases this phenomenon. Interestingly, Section 2 points out that the monotheizing of Hebrew Scripture, its collapsing of all Mesopotamian god-characters into the one biblical god, is not at all straightforward or evenhanded. Yhwh ends up looking far more like *one* character from the Atrahasis Epic, the grieving mother goddess Nintu, than like the other and angrier characters.

The next two case studies each in their own way present the other "mode" of monotheizing: not aggregative but *evacuative*. According to this mode, the parts and powers of other characters are not added into the biblical god. Instead, the powers of other characters, their privileges and safety, are subtracted. They are rendered far less, transformed from self-determined, self-standing agents into objects of the supreme god's discretion. Section 3 thus inspects the relative privilege and protection of the god's beloved, kingly son in some ancient (and some biblical) texts, in order to show how Psalm 89 depicts Yhwh's extraordinary and scandalous aggression against his own king. Section 4 examines the Golden Calf story in Exodus 32–34 and argues that Yhwh's threat of annihilating the whole people of Israel corresponds to the text's covenantal framing: the people's status as treasured possession is endangered because of their sworn oath to serve Yhwh exclusively – and because of his imperial sovereignty over their life and death.

Each of these latter two sections also traces out the ways that subsequent Jewish and Christian readers did not reprise the monotheizing of Hebrew Scripture. Rather, in their various inflections, they *relaxed* the concentration of all divine powers into a single god. They let other characters resume their agency, their privilege and safety. They repopulated the heavenlies such that powers and principalities, angels and archangels, blurred the boundary line between God and humanity that the Hebrew Scriptures, by and large, maintain. They gave God a host of deputies and opponents, with the result that, in some cases, the complex and composite divine biblical character recedes; the God of the Book of Watchers is (for instance) a far less conflicted individual than the God of the Genesis Flood Story. He is also less destructive, since his angelic underlings and not he himself prosecute the cleansing of the world by a flood. Or, again, these later reading traditions made God's Beloved Son once again impervious, exempting him absolutely from any threat of divine aggression. Indeed, far from vulnerability to them, this divine scion holds the keys to death and hell (Rev 1:18)! These later readers built the people of God into the very body of the *christos*; and "No one ever hates his own body, but he nourishes and tenderly cares for it" (Eph 5:29). In these ways, the traditions that received the Hebrew Bible as scripture de-monotheized. Insofar as monotheizing, considered as a textual procedure, *intensified* aggression, de-monotheizing textually redistributed it, with the effect of tempering and reducing it.[95]

Section 1 of the present Element took an agnostic position concerning both the historical conditions that inspired the Hebrew Bible's monotheizing and concerning the subsequent sources of Jewish and Christian de-monotheizing. It aspired to a textual approach, not seeking to move through and beyond the relevant texts to their historical authors and audiences, let alone to their inner thoughts, but remaining at the textual level in terms of observation and argument. Yet the historical questions intrude. If it be proved that they did so, why did Hebrew Scripture, or significant portions thereof, literarily aggregate divine powers into the one god, Yhwh? Why, relative both to its theological forebears *and* to its aftercomers, is the Hebrew Bible such an outlier in its concentration of divine roles and powers – an intellectual interlude, but one with canonical standing for multiple worshipping communities? In the face of its example, why did early Jewish and Christian readers repopulate the divine world? There may be no grand unified theory that answers any of these questions. But more specific, granular answers may well lie within historians' reach.

Section 1 also indicated the present work's historical ambit. Although its content is theological, it is in a nontechnical sense: it does not launch constructive arguments about the real, extratextual God. This study restricts itself to the textual god only, considered as an artifact of intellectual and literary history. In this way, the book is (I hope) engaging and accessible both to critics and confessors of the biblical god. The whole work is meant neither as a critique nor as a defense of him. Perhaps dissident or defensive moments slip in, crypto-indignation or crypto-apologia. But the book does not seek to reason from biblical texts toward the living and present God to whom religious traditions believe the texts give witness. Nonetheless, for some readers, this matter presses urgently. And to be honest, it does for me, too. How does divine aggression, especially if it is distinctively ferocious in the Bible, map onto the living God? How might biblical portraiture, even of Yhwh's destructiveness, shape current-day theological claims

---

[95] Again, as with footnote 70: the *textual* strictures of the book's argument must be remembered, and its historical and comparative coordinates. It does not arbitrate the divinity of Christ, it registers observations about the rendering of literary characters, especially Yhwh, his king, and his people, their relative power over one another and safety from one another.

and expectations? What ways are there of reinhabiting or rehabilitating biblical accounts of God's opposition, even God's destructive power?

These kinds of questions go beyond the purview of this book (also beyond my earlier monograph from Cambridge University Press).[96] But they belong in its ellipse. It is here that the category of therapeutic aggression, which Section 1 introduced, might serve as an entrée or lens. It seems clear that a few biblical texts envision divine aggression as a mysterious and painful *prelude* to divine beneficence, an occasion or an antechamber: so it was with Jacob at the Jabbok (Gen 32) or Isaiah's call (Isa 6). These therapeutic texts are, admittedly, a minority report within the welter of Hebrew Bible passages where the rhetorical purpose of divine aggression is to catalyze fear, dread, and avoidance, and nothing more complicated or ultimate, at least on the near textual horizon. But even so, these texts suggest an interpretive direction that may find broader, constructive applicability: divine destructiveness layered into divine healing; Gehenna hidden within the Kingdom of God (Isaac of Nineveh).[97]

So, too, the larger question of monotheism and monotheizing, which the Elements series aims to enrich: how can divine aggression complicate or fill in larger scholarly discourse about monotheism? I suspect the present Element offers at least the following lessons, both, in their own way, cautionary. First, highlighting increased aggression as an effect of monotheizing shows a potential *cost* of this theological move. Treating one god alone as god offers intellectual and spiritual advantages, to be sure. It assures that one god deals out weal and woe alike – and it is *the god whom one knows* and no stranger. "Faithful are the wounds of a friend; but the kisses of an enemy are deceitful" (Prov 27:6 NKJV). This is one powerful logic that may inform monotheizing: even if Yhwh exacts harm, at least it is the wounds of a friend. But this monotheizing literary strategy also brings intellectual and spiritual costs. The character of that singular god becomes more ambiguous, more violent. We inheritors of such traditions are left accepting both good and evil from the same hands (compare Job: "Shall we receive good from God and not receive evil?" [2:10]). For many theologians and believers, this may be too high a price to pay.[98]

Second, the departure of postbiblical Jewish and Christian theologies from monotheizing biblical templates may constitute a historic, lived example of refusal to pay that price. Such a claim cannot be verified apart from detailed

---

[96] Cornell, *Divine Aggression*.

[97] Brock, ed., *The Second Part*, XXXIX (162–173); see further Hryrniewicz, "Universalism of Salvation."

[98] Compare Römer, "Yhwh, the Goddess, and Evil," especially p. 4 on "Yhwh, creator of good and evil."

examination of particular biblical texts, their reception, and the worlds of Second Temple Judaism and the Hellenistic Near East. But even before and apart from that legwork, the fact remains: the communities that laid claim to the literature of Hebrew Scripture did not reproduce its (literary) monotheizing. They let its theological model lie fallow. This should caution modern-day advocates of monotheism. Why was it, at least as a literary phenomenon, a distribution of divine powers on the page, unsustainable? Were the factors that led to an embrace of a different theological configuration (like, say, apocalyptic dualism) so different from those that current-day religious communities face?

Finally, the introductory section of the present Element promised to touch on one juncture at which the arguments of recent books on monotheism and violence intersect its own about monotheizing and aggression.[99] Whereas these works track the costs of monotheism on *other* (non-monotheist) human communities, the preceding paragraphs name the potential cost of monotheizing on the inheritors of the Bible's monotheizing rhetoric. These are distinct: the harms experienced by victims of monotheism versus the quandaries faced by devotees of the friend-wounding, good-and-evil-wielding biblical god. Yet they may bear some relation, perhaps even a concentric one, as of the inner ring to the outer. That is, among the possible historical reasons for movement *away* from the Hebrew Bible's monotheizing rhetoric and *toward* poly-sovereign rhetorics of early Judaism and Christianity could be: hesitation about the price of the omni-sovereign *on religious neighbors*, in addition to one's own community. A god who is capable of withdrawing favor and protection from his very own king and his very own treasured people – this is a god who jeopardizes other nations also and all the more (see the biblical Oracles against the Nations), and the same reasoning that evidently persuaded some tradents of the Hebrew Bible to shore up the status and sovereignty of Yhwh's king and people might have catalyzed a reassessment of other peoples, too. The inspirations for de-monotheizing might, in other words, have ramified beyond Israel and claimants to Israel. If so – and again, verification would require further serious historical research – then the argument of the present Element would adjoin these other recent books, but it would have the effect of moving the "cost-counting" *inside of* the traditions that inherit the Hebrew Bible. The "price of monotheism," on Yhwh's own people *and* on other peoples, might already have been calculated by early Jews and Christians and not only by late modern critics of monotheism.[100]

---

[99] These books include Assmann, *Price of Monotheism*; Bettini, *In Praise of Polytheism*; and Schwartz, *Curse of Cain.*

[100] 4 Ezra is an important datum in this regard, especially chapter 7.

Bibliography

Aaron, David H. *Etched in Stone: The Emergence of the Decalogue.* London: T&T Clark, 2006.

Aberbach, Moshe and Levi Smolar. "Aaron, Jereboam, and the Golden Calves." *JBL* 86 (1967): 129–140.

Angel, Hayyim. "The Eternal Davidic Covenant in II Samuel Chapter 7 and Its Later Manifestation in the Bible." *JBQ* 44 (2016): 83–90.

Baloian, Bruce. *Anger in the Old Testament.* AUS 99. New York: Peter Lang, 1992.

Berges, Ulrich. "Der Zorn Gottes in der Prophetie und Poesie Israels auf dem Hintergrund altorientalischer Vorstellungen." *Bib* 85 (2004): 305–340.

Blum, Erhard. "Urgeschichte." *TRE* 34 (2002): 436–445.

Brock, Sebastian, ed. *Isaac of Nineveh (Isaac the Syrian), The Second Part; Chapters IV–XLI. Corpus scriptorum christianorum orientalium 554–555/ Scriptores Syri 224–225.* Leuven: Peeters, 1995.

Carr, David M. *The Formation of Genesis 1–11: Biblical and Other Precursors.* New York: Oxford University Press, 2020.

Chapman, Stephen B. *The Law and the Prophets: A Study in Old Testament Canon Formation.* FAT 27. Tübingen: Mohr Siebeck, 2000.

Chapman, Stephen B. "*Miqreh* and YHWH: Fate, Chance, Simultaneity, and Providence." In *Divine Doppelgängers: YHWH's Ancient Look-Alikes,* edited by Collin Cornell, 181–200. University Park, PA: Eisenbrauns/Penn State University Press, 2020.

Childs, Brevard S. *The Book of Exodus: A Critical, Theological Commentary.* OTL. Philadelphia, PA: Westminster Press, 1974.

Clifford, Richard J. "Psalm 89: A Lament over the Davidic Ruler's Continued Failure." *HTR* 73 (1980): 35–47.

Clines, David. "Noah's Flood I: The Theology of the Flood Narrative." *Faith and Thought* 100 (1972–3): 128–142.

Considine, Patrick. "The Theme of Divine Wrath in Ancient East Mediterranean Literature." *SMEA* 8 (1969): 85–109.

Cornell, Collin. *Divine Aggression in Psalms and Inscriptions: Vengeful Gods and Loyal Kings.* SOTS. Cambridge: Cambridge University Press, 2021.

Cornell, Collin. "The Royal Psalms, or: The King in the Psalms." In *Cambridge Companion to the Psalms,* edited by Brent A. Strawn and Joel M. LeMon. Cambridge: Cambridge University Press, forthcoming.

Cornell, Collin. "The Value of Egyptian Aramaic for Biblical Studies." *Journal of Biblical and Theological Studies* 7 (2022): 3–19.

Davies, Philip R. "And Enoch Was Not, for Genesis Took Him." In *Biblical Traditions in Transmission: Essays in Honour of Michael A. Knibb*, edited by Charlotte Hempel, 97–107. JSJSup 111. Leiden: Brill, 2006.

Day, John. "Comparative Ancient Near Eastern Study: The Genesis Flood Narrative in Relation to Ancient Near Eastern Flood Accounts." In *Biblical Interpretation and Method: Essays in Honour of John Barton*, edited by Katharine J. Dell and Paul M. Joyce, 74–88. Oxford: Oxford University Press, 2013.

deClaissé-Walford, Nancy, ed. *The Shape and Shaping of the Book of Psalms: The Current State of Scholarship*. AIL 20. Atlanta, GA: SBL Press, 2014.

Draffkorn Kilmer, Anne. "The Mesopotamian Concept of Overpopulation and Its Solution As Reflected in the Mythology." *Or* 41 (1972): 160–177.

Fox, Everett. *The Five Books of Moses: Genesis, Exodus, Leviticus, Numbers, Deuteronomy: A New Translation with Introductions, Commentary, and Notes*. Schocken Bible 1. New York: Schocken, 1995.

Frankena, Rintje. "The Vassal-Treaties of Esarhaddon and the Dating of Deuteronomy." In *Kaf-Hē: 1940–1965 Jubilee Volume, Published on the Occasion of the 25th Anniversary of the Dutch O. T. Society*, edited by Pieter Arie Hendrik de Boer, 122–154. OtSt 14. Leiden: Brill, 1965.

Fredriksen, Paula. "Mandatory Retirement: Ideas in the Study of Christian Origins Whose Time Has Come to Go." *SR* 35 (2006): 231–246.

George, Andrew, trans. *The Epic of Gilgamesh*. London: Penguin Press, 1999.

Goldenberg, Robert. "Why Should the Look-Alikes Be a Problem?" In *Divine Doppelgängers: YHWH's Ancient Look-Alikes*, edited by Collin Cornell, 88–96. University Park, PA: Eisenbrauns/Penn State University Press, 2020.

Grant, Deena A. *Divine Anger in the Hebrew Bible*. CBQMS 52. Washington, DC: Catholic Biblical Association of America, 2014.

Green, Douglas J. *"I Undertook Great Works": The Ideology of Domestic Achievements in West Semitic Royal Inscriptions*. FAT 2.41. Tübingen: Mohr Siebeck, 2010.

Greenberg, Moshe. "Hebrew *segulla*: Akkadian *sikiltu*." *JAOS* 71 (1951): 172–174.

Hay, David M. *Glory at the Right Hand: Psalm 110 in Early Christianity*. SBLMS 18. Nashville, TN: Abingdon, 1973.

Hayes, Christine E. "Golden Calf Stories: The Relationship of Exodus 32 and Deuteronomy 9–10." In *The Idea of Biblical Interpretation: Essays in Honor of James L. Kugel*, edited by Hindy Najman and Judith Newman, 45–93. JSJSup 83. Leiden: Brill, 2004.

Henze, Matthias. *Mind the Gap: How the Jewish Writings between the Old and New Testament Help Us Understand Jesus*. Minneapolis, MN: Fortress Press, 2017.

Hryrniewicz, Wacław. "Universalism of Salvation: St, Isaac The Syrian." In *Die Wurzel aller Theologie: Sentire Cum Ecclesia, Festschrift zum 60 Geburstag von Urs Von Arx*, edited by Hans Gerny, Harald Rein, and Maja Weyermann, 139–150. Bern: Stämpfli, 2003.

Humphreys, W. Lee. *The Character of God in the Book of Genesis*. Louisville, KT: Westminster John Knox, 2001.

Jacobsen, Thorkild. "The Eridu Genesis." In *I Studied Inscriptions from Before the Flood: Ancient Near Eastern, Literary, and Linguistic Approaches to Genesis 1–11*, edited by Richard S. Hess and David Toshio Tsumura, 129–142. SBTSOTS 4. Winona Lake, IN: Eisenbrauns, 1994.

Käsemann, Ernst. "The Theological Problem Presented by the Motif of the Body of Christ." In *Perspectives on Paul*, 102–121. Translated by Margaret Kohl. Philadelphia, PA: Fortress, 1971.

Keel, Othmar. "Yahweh as Mother Goddess." *Theology Digest* 36 (1989): 233–236.

Kratz, Reinhard G. and Hermann Spieckermann, eds. *Divine Wrath and Divine Mercy in the World of Antiquity*. FAT 33. Tübingen: Mohr Siebeck, 2008.

Kugler, Gili. "Metaphysical Hatred and Sacred Genocide: The Questionable Role of Amalek in Biblical Literature." *Journal of Genocide Research* 23 (2021): 1–16.

Kugler, Gili. *When God Wanted to Destroy the Chosen People: Biblical Traditions and Theology on the Move*. BZAW 515. Berlin: De Gruyter, 2019.

Lam, Joseph. "Psalm 2 and the Disinheritance of Earthly Rulers: New Light from the Ugaritic Legal Text RS 94.2168." *VT* 64 (2014): 34–46.

Lambert, Wilfred G. *Babylonian Creation Myths*. Mesopotamian Civilizations 16. Winona Lake, IN: Eisenbrauns, 2013.

Lambert, Wilfred G. and Alan R. Millard, *Atra-Hasis: the Babylonian Story of the Flood*. Oxford: Clarendon, 1970.

Lang, Martin. "Floating from Babylon to Rome: Ancient Near Eastern Flood Stories in the Mediterranean World." *Kaskal* 5 (2008): 211–231.

Lawson, Jack N. *The Concept of Fate in Ancient Mesopotamia of the First Millennium: Toward an Understanding of Šīmtu*. Orientalia Biblica et Christiana 7. Wiesbaden: Harrassowitz, 1994.

Mendenhall, George E. "Covenant Forms in Israelite Tradition." *BA* 17 (1954): 49–76.

Miles, Jack. *God: A Biography*. New York: Alfred A. Knopf, 1995.

Milik, J. T. *The Books of Enoch: Aramaic Fragments of Qumrân Cave 4.* Oxford: Clarendon, 1976.

Moberly, R. W. L. "How Appropriate Is 'Monotheism' as a Category for Biblical Interpretation?" In *Early Jewish and Christian Monotheism*, edited by Loren T. Stuckenbruck and Wendy E. S. North, 216–234. JSNTSup 263. London: T&T Clark, 2004.

Moberly, R. W. L. *The God of the Old Testament: Encountering the Divine in Christian Scripture.* Grand Rapids, MI: Baker Academic, 2020.

Nicholson, Ernest W. *God and His People: Covenant and Theology in the Old Testament.* New York: Oxford University Press, 1986.

Nickelsburg, George W. E. and James C. VanderKam. *1 Enoch: The Hermeneia Translation.* Minneapolis, MN: Fortress, 2012.

Novenson, Matthew V. *The Grammar of Messianism: An Ancient Jewish Political Idiom and Its Users.* New York: Oxford University Press, 2017.

Olyan, Saul M. "Is Isaiah 40–55 Really Monotheistic?" *JANER* 12 (2012): 190–201.

Otto, Eckart. *Das Deuteronomium: Politische Theologie und Rechtsreform in Juda und Assyrien.* BZAW 284. Berlin: De Gruyter, 1999.

Parpola, Simo and Kazuko Watanabe. *Neo-Assyrian Treaties and Loyalty Oaths.* SAA 2. Helsinki: Helsinki University Press, 1988.

Payne, Annick. *Iron Age Hieroglyphic Luwian Inscriptions.* WAW 29. Atlanta, GA: Society of Biblical Literature, 2012.

Pettinato, G. "Die Bestrafung des Menschengeschlechts durch die Sintflut: Die erste Tafel des Atramḫasīs-Epos eröffnet eine neue Einsicht in die Motivation dieser Strafe." *Or* 37 (1968): 165–200.

Prinsloo, Gert T. M. "Reading the Masoretic Psalter as a Book: Editorial Trends and Redactional Trajectories." *CurBR* 19 (2021): 145–177.

Römer, Thomas C. "Yhwh, the Goddess, and Evil: Is 'Monotheism' an Adequate Concept to Describe the Hebrew Bible's Discourses about the God of Israel?" *Verbum et Ecclesia* 34 (2013): 1–5.

Sanders, James A. *The Monotheizing Process: Its Origins and Development.* Eugene, OR: Cascade, 2014.

Schlimm, Matthew R. *From Fratricide to Forgiveness: The Language and Ethics of Anger in Genesis.* Siphrut 7. Winona Lake, IN: Eisenbrauns, 2011.

Schlimm, Matthew R. Review of Deena Grant, *Divine Anger in the Hebrew Bible. JHS* 15 (2015). https://doi.org/10.5508/jhs.2015.v15.r8

Sommer, Benjamin D. "Yehezkel Kaufmann and Recent Scholarship: Toward a Richer Discourse of Monotheism." In *Yehezkel Kaufmann and the Reinvention of Jewish Biblical Scholarship*, ed. Job Y. Jindo, Benjamin

D. Sommer, and Thomas Staubli, 204–239. OBO 283. Göttingen: Vandenhoeck & Ruprecht, 2017.

Sonnet, Jean-Pierre. "God's Repentance and 'False Starts' In Biblical History (Genesis 6–9; Exodus 32–34; 1 Samuel 15 And 2 Samuel 7)." In *Congress Volume Ljubljana 2007*, ed. André Lemaire, 469–494. VTSup 133. Leiden: Brill, 2009.

Starbuck, Scott R. A. "Theological Anthropology at a Fulcrum: Isaiah 55:1–5, Psalm 89, and Second Stage *Traditio* in the Royal Psalms." In *David and Zion: Biblical Studies in Honor of J. J. M. Roberts*, ed. Bernard F. Batto and Kathryn L. Roberts, 247–265. Winona Lake, IN: Eisenbrauns, 2004.

Strawn, Brent A. "Yhwh's Poesie: The *Gnadenformel*, the Book of Exodus, and Beyond." In *The Incomparable God: Readings in Biblical Theology*, ed. Collin Cornell and M. Justin Walker, 26–44. Grand Rapids, MI: Eerdmans, 2023.

Suriano, Matthew J. "The Apology of Hazael: A Literary and Historical Analysis of the Tel Dan Inscription." *JNES* 66 (2007): 163–176.

Thompson, John Arthur. *The Ancient Near Eastern Treaties and the Old Testament*. London: Tyndale, 1964.

Thompson, Thomas L. "A Testimony of the Good King: Reading the Mesha Stele." In *Ahab Agonistes: The Rise and Fall of the Omri Dynasty*, ed. Lester L. Grabbe, 236–292. LHBOTS 421/ESHM 6. London: T&T Clark, 2007.

Tolan, Patrick H. "Understanding Violence." In *The Cambridge Handbook of Violent Behavior and Aggression*, ed. Daniel J. Flannery, Alexander T. Vazsonyi, and Irwin D. Waldman, 5–18. Cambridge: Cambridge University Press, 2007.

Tropper, Josef. *Die Inschriften von Zincirli: Neue Edition und vergleichende Grammatik des phönizischen, sam'alischen und aramäischen Textkorpus*. Abhandlungen zur Literatur Alt-Syrien-Palästinas 6. Münster: Ugarit-Verlag, 1993.

Volf, Miroslav. "Divine Violence?" *ChrC* 116 (1999): 972.

Von Soden, Wolfram. "Der Mensch bescheidet sich nicht Überlegungen zu Schöpfungserzählungen in Babylonien und Israel." In *Bibel und Alter Orient: Altorientalische Beiträge zum Alten Testament*, edited by Hans-Peter Müller. BZAW 162. Berlin: De Gruyter, 1995.

Wälchli, Stefan H. *Gottes Zorn in den Psalmen: eine Studie zur Rede vom Zorn Gottes in den Psalmen im Kontext des Alten Testaments*. OBO 244. Göttingen: Vandenhoeck & Ruprecht; Academic Press, 2012.

Walker, Justin. *The Power of Images: The Poetics of Violence in Lamentations 2 and Ancient Near Eastern Art*. OBO 297. Leuven: Peeters, 2022.

Wasserman, Nathan. *The Flood: The Akkadian Sources – A New Edition, Commentary, and a Literary Discussion*. OBO 290. Leuven: Peeters, 2020.

Weinfeld, Moshe. "Traces of Assyrian Treaty Formulae in Deuteronomy." *Bib* 46 (1965): 417–427.

Wilson, Gerald H. *The Editing of the Hebrew Psalter*. SBLDS 76. Chico, CA: Scholars Press, 1985.

Wilson, Gerald H. "King, Messiah, and the Reign of God: Revisiting the Royal Psalms and the Shape of the Psalter." In *The Book of Psalms: Composition and Reception*, edited by Peter W. Flint and Patrick D., Miller, Jr. 391–406. VTSup 99. Leiden: Brill, 2005.

Wyatt, Nicolas. "The Evidence of the Colophons in the Assessment of Ilimilku's Scribal and Authorial Role." *UF* 46 (2015): 399–446.

Cambridge Elements ⁼

Religion and Monotheism

Paul K. Moser
Loyola University Chicago
Paul K. Moser is Professor of Philosophy at Loyola University Chicago. He is the author of *Paul's Gospel of Divine Self-Sacrifice; The Divine Goodness of Jesus; Divine Guidance; Understanding Religious Experience; The God Relationship; The Elusive God* (winner of national book award from the Jesuit Honor Society); *The Evidence for God; The Severity of God; Knowledge and Evidence* (all Cambridge University Press); and *Philosophy after Objectivity* (Oxford University Press); co-author of *Theory of Knowledge* (Oxford University Press); editor of *Jesus and Philosophy* (Cambridge University Press) and *The Oxford Handbook of Epistemology* (Oxford University Press); co-editor of *The Wisdom of the Christian Faith* (Cambridge University Press). He is the co-editor with Chad Meister of the book series *Cambridge Studies in Religion, Philosophy, and Society*.

Chad Meister
Affiliate Scholar, Ansari Institute for Global Engagement with Religion, University of Notre Dame
Chad Meister is Affiliate Scholar at the Ansari Institute for Global Engagement with Religion at the University of Notre Dame. His authored and co-authored books include *Evil: A Guide for the Perplexed* (Bloomsbury Academic, 2ⁿᵈ edition); *Introducing Philosophy of Religion* (Routledge); *Introducing Christian Thought* (Routledge, 2ⁿᵈ edition); and *Contemporary Philosophical Theology* (Routledge). He has edited or co-edited the following: *The Oxford Handbook of Religious Diversity* (Oxford University Press); *Debating Christian Theism* (Oxford University Press); with Paul Moser, *The Cambridge Companion to the Problem of Evil* (Cambridge University Press); and with Charles Taliaferro, *The History of Evil* (Routledge, in six volumes). He is the co-editor with Paul Moser of the book series *Cambridge Studies in Religion, Philosophy, and Society*.

About the Series
This Cambridge Element series publishes original concise volumes on monotheism and its significance. Monotheism has occupied inquirers since the time of the Biblical patriarch, and it continues to attract interdisciplinary academic work today. Engaging, current, and concise, the Elements benefit teachers, researched, and advanced students in religious studies, Biblical studies, theology, philosophy of religion, and related fields.

Cambridge Elements $\equiv$

Religion and Monotheism

Printed in the United States
by Baker & Taylor Publisher Services